natural *style*

Using Organic and Eco-Conscious Materials for Earth-Friendly Designs

Janet Sobesky

CRE▲TIVE
HOMEOWNER®

CREATIVE
HOMEOWNER®

Natural Style
Vice President-Content: Christopher Reggio
Editor: Colleen Dorsey
Copy Editor: Jeremy Hauck
Technical Editor: Karen Lanier
Designer: Wendy Reynolds
Indexer: Elizabeth Walker

ISBN 978-1-58011-829-3

Library of Congress Cataloging-in-Publication Data

Names: Sobesky, Janet, author.
Title: Natural style / Janet Sobesky.
Description: Mount Joy : Creative Homeowner, 2019. | Includes index.
Identifiers: LCCN 2018033076 (print) | LCCN 2018034500 (ebook) | ISBN
  9781607656586 | ISBN 9781580118293
Subjects: LCSH: Interior decoration--Environmental aspects. | Green products.
Classification: LCC NK2113 (ebook) | LCC NK2113 .S63 2019 (print) | DDC
  747--dc23
LC record available at https://lccn.loc.gov/2018033076

We are always looking for talented authors. To submit an idea, please send a brief inquiry
to acquisitions@foxchapelpublishing.com.

Printed in Singapore

Current Printing (last digit)
10 9 8 7 6 5 4 3 2 1

Creative Homeowner®, *www.creativehomeowner.com*, is an imprint of New Design Originals
Corporation and distributed exclusively in North America by Fox Chapel Publishing
Company, Inc., 800-457-9112, 903 Square Street, Mount Joy, PA 17552, and in the United
Kingdom by Grantham Book Service, Trent Road, Grantham, Lincolnshire, NG31 7XQ.

Dedication

To my husband, Brent, for his unwavering enthusiasm
and belief in me, and for my mother, who taught me
to appreciate the beauty in simple things.

Acknowledgments

Special thanks to Martha Olandese for her superb research and
writing assistance. Thanks also to David Bergman, architect and
sustainable design expert, for sharing his wisdom with me.

Thanks to the National Kitchen and Bath Association, the National
Association of Remodeling Industries, and the color experts at
Benjamin Moore, Glidden, and Pantone for guidance and information.

Thanks to Lisa Kahn and Kathie Robitz for their editing expertise.

Note

Although this book is written primarily for a U.S. audience, it contains
useful information for readers in any country. Information and
websites about laws, guidelines, and products specific to the
U.S. may not apply to all readers, but can provide a
good starting point for further local research.

Contents

Introduction

A HOME SHOULD BE A SAFE HAVEN—a place where you and your loved ones not only live, but also thrive. Decorating naturally lets you accomplish that. Natural style is more than interior design; it's a commitment to comfort, simplicity, and materials that are good for your family and the earth. On these pages, you'll learn how to create a beautiful, eco-friendly home. You'll also find information and inspiration that will help you choose natural products to suit your needs, taste, and budget.

CHAPTER 1

What Is *Natural Style?*

Reflecting nature's beauty in your home

Your home is both your retreat and your door to the world. It is where you raise your children, continue family traditions, and spend time with friends and relatives. Your home is part of a larger community. It reflects who you are and what you find meaningful. Your personal style is what makes your home a peaceful, healthy, relaxing environment.

BECAUSE THE HEALTH AND HAPPINESS of the people who share your home are so precious to you, natural style is a logical choice. It's a look that's simple and soothing. It's not over the top or subject to the whims of the latest style gurus or trendsetters. The essence of natural style is achieving more with less, removing clutter and excessive ornamentation, and highlighting quality materials and objects that have personal significance.

When you choose natural style, your rooms aren't showy stage sets, but comfortable backdrops for everyday life. The use of natural materials, such as cotton, linen, wood, and stone, comes from a desire to fill your home with the beauty of the outdoors. But natural style is about more than shunning flashiness and synthetic fabrics; it's also a commitment to selecting products that are healthy for your family, as well as for the earth.

OPPOSITE The unexpected juxtaposition of colors and materials in this natural-style dining area is both eye-catching and serenely comfortable.

The Global Environment

Your connection to nature is reflected in your actions, which include how you treat the environment and how the environment is reflected in your home. The amount of energy you use, the products you buy, and the way you dispose of them all make an impact on the air, water, and land. So, too, do the construction materials used to build our homes, the chemicals emitted by the finishes on our walls and cabinetry, and the pollution created when certain household goods are manufactured. Focusing our attention on these critical issues makes us aware of the need for ecologically safe and responsible choices inside our own homes.

BELOW A combination of materials, textures, and shapes tempts the senses. Further interest is added by combining matte finishes with highly reflective materials and the natural with the man-made.

Climate Change

The earth's average surface temperature is on the rise. Greenhouse gases such as carbon dioxide (CO_2), carbon monoxide, methane, and nitrous oxide are emitted into the air when fossil fuels such as coal,

LEFT Memoirs from vacations and family outings can be integrated into a natural-style décor, reminding all of shared memories.

oil, and natural gas are burned to generate electricity, heat homes, power factories, and run cars. Global warming is the impact that greenhouse gases have on the atmosphere, causing changes in climate worldwide. Locally, impacts range from droughts to flooding, more severe storms, rising sea levels, and less snow and ice, resulting in changes in animal migration patterns and plant life cycles.

While this may seem like an insurmountable issue, everyone can make an impact by choosing natural products, materials, and finishes and by maintaining a home in an eco-friendly manner.

ABOVE A candlelit chandelier conserves electricity and provides a cozy and romantic touch to meals.

Use of Less Energy

Much of the greenhouse gases emitted into the environment come from cars and energy usage. You can get an idea of your carbon footprint by using the EPA's online calculator (*www3.epa.gov/carbon-footprint-calculator*) to assess your home energy, waste, and transportation. Your local extension offices or utility provider may have programs and incentives for conducting an energy audit to find out where improvements can be made in the home. You can download a free energy guide as well (*www.energy.gov*). Simple fixes include teaching children not to leave a trail of lights on behind them, using dimmers and timers on lights, sealing cracks around electrical outlets and plumbing fixtures, and using power strips to turn off electronics at night. In 2012, new lighting standards went into effect so that more energy efficient light bulbs are commonly available for household use. Other proactive strategies include placing windows or skylights to maximize natural light and heat from the sun; properly insulating the attic, crawl spaces, water heater, and pipes; and seeking help from a professional certified by the Building Performance Institute (BPI, *www.bpihomeowner.org*).

When purchasing new or used appliances, look for the Energy Star label. This designation means that they use less energy, which reduces greenhouse gas emissions and air pollution. Keep your heating and cooling systems in tip-top condition by servicing them regularly. Install a whole-house fan to cool your house overnight in lieu of the air conditioner. If you are not using the television, radio, or another appliance, turn it off. A microwave oven uses less energy than the stove to heat small meals. Consider an on-demand water heater instead of the standard tank model, which wastes energy heating water when it's not being used. Dry your laundry outdoors instead of using a clothes dryer.

There may also be some passive energy-saving techniques you can use in your home design and landscape. For example, awnings and deciduous trees on the southern exposure provide shade in the summer; when leaves fall and awnings are rolled back, they welcome the sun's heat into your home in the winter. Tile flooring absorbs warmth when exposed to the sun through energy-efficient skylights or south-facing windows. Use cross ventilation, screen doors, and ceiling fans to increase airflow and help keep your home cool in warmer months.

Reduce, Reuse, Recycle, and Respond

Simply giving a second life to what you already own can help to reduce greenhouse gases. Go beyond recycling. You can make the choice to reduce, reuse, recycle, and respond. That includes reducing the amount of trash we discard, reusing containers and other products, recycling household materials and compost, and responding

LIVE WISE, LIVE WELL

Recycling Savvy

Are you tired of watching that old car battery, outdated telephone, and nonworking TV gather dust in your garage? At least half of U.S. states require you to recycle electronics, and many have banned them from landfills. Many cities and counties offer e-waste drop-off events around Earth Day each year (April 22). There are ways to recycle nearly everything these days; the trick is discovering how and where. A great place to begin is the website Earth911 (*www.earth911.com*), which offers comprehensive local recycling information by zip code.

LEFT "Passed down from my relatives" doesn't have to be a bad thing. This well-worn mantel, table, and chair lend tremendous character and style and don't add to any landfills.

to the problem of solid waste disposal with changes in our preferences and buying habits. Don't throw out items unnecessarily—consider repairing or repurposing what you have. If you need to dispose of things, donate them to charity. Compost yard waste, grass clippings, food scraps, and coffee grounds.

When shopping, check places such as Goodwill, the Salvation Army, garage sales, Habitat for Humanity's ReStore, and even Grandma's house for previously owned products. You'll save money and might end up with high-quality household items. When purchasing new products, look for green choices such as solid wood furniture, rechargeable batteries, and eco-friendly cleaners. A home with less clutter is likely to be less harmful to the environment.

Deforestation

In addition to their beauty and the many products they provide, trees trap carbon and other particles produced by pollution. Unfortunately, billions of acres of forests around the world have been destroyed to

BELOW This distinctive outdoor room is built with local, biodegradable, and renewable materials.

meet the ever-increasing demand for exotic woods, farmland, and industrial growth. An average of 80,000 acres of tropical rainforest is destroyed on a daily basis, along with the diverse plants and animals that live there. This deforestation decreases overall air quality because it releases billions of tons of carbon into the air and kills the largest air purifiers on the planet: trees. You can help by carefully considering the origin of the wood products you buy. Is it from a renewable resource? Does it support indigenous peoples? Naturally, it also makes sense to use recycled wood whenever possible.

Waste

While almost every community has some type of recycling program in place, sometimes it's hard to tell what can go in the recycling bin and what is trash meant for the landfill. For a list of recyclables, contact your local recycling office.

Solid Waste

Millions of tons of waste materials are produced during the manufacturing and use of consumer products. Much of this consists of plastics and discarded packaging. In 2015, approximately 262 million tons of trash was thrown out of American homes. That's nearly

4.5 pounds of garbage per person per day. About a quarter of all the waste was recycled, and more than half of it was trucked to landfills. Much of this waste isn't biodegradable and some of it produces toxic residue that pollutes the soil and water. If possible, choose products with minimal packaging, as well as long-lasting items that wear well and look better with age. Purchase products made with reclaimed materials or recycled plastics, or simply reduce the amount of products you buy.

Household Hazardous Waste

The average home can accumulate as much as 100 pounds (45 kilograms) of hazardous waste in the basement, the garage, and storage closets. The list of hazardous substances includes common items such as toilet, drain, and oven cleaners, batteries, wood preservatives, oil-based paints, and flea repellants and shampoos for pets. Check to see if there is a safe disposal program for these items in your community or at a local business. (Some garages or automotive supply companies accept used oil or car batteries.) And did you know that some old electronic devices such as MP3 players and cell phones contain lead, chromium, and mercury? Try "e-cycling" these devices. The Electronic Industries Alliance E-Cycling website (*www.eiae.org*) compiles a list of nationwide e-cyclers by zip code.

What's Inside Your Home?

Your home is more than a roof over your family's head. It should provide a safe and healthy sanctuary from excessive noise, dirt, and harmful fumes.

Indoor Air Quality

In an effort to reduce heating and cooling costs, many "airtight" homes have been constructed over the past 50 years. Unfortunately, this resulted in a buildup of indoor contaminants like mold and carbon monoxide. In fact, studies have shown that the air inside our homes can be more polluted than the outdoor air in some big cities. Infants, the elderly, and people with chronic respiratory, cardiovascular, and immune diseases can be especially vulnerable to these pollutants.

The rate at which outdoor air replaces indoor air is described as the air-exchange rate. When there is little infiltration of outdoor air through natural or mechanical ventilation, the air-exchange rate is low and pollutant levels can increase. Factors that contribute to bad indoor air include tobacco smoke; construction materials; paints, stains, and finishes on walls, floors, cabinets, and furniture; and activities such as cooking, heating, cooling, and cleaning. An upswing of respiratory illnesses and allergic reactions may also show up soon after exposure to some indoor air pollutants. Long-term exposure could lead to severely debilitating problems such as asthma, heart disease, and cancer. The EPA says the most effective ways to improve your indoor air quality are to remove the sources of pollutants and to ventilate with clean outdoor air. Improving air movement within your home can be as simple as opening windows and doors and installing ceiling fans.

Combustion Gases

Combustion is a major source of indoor air pollutants. Particles or gases that result from appliances that burn fuels include gas ranges and ovens, space heaters, gas water heaters, wood- or coal-burning stoves, and fireplaces. These appliances create combustion pollutants from burning natural or LP gas, fuel oil, kerosene, wood, or coal. Some of the pollutants that result are carbon monoxide, nitrogen dioxide, sulfur dioxide, unburned hydrocarbons, and aldehydes.

Exposure to combustion pollution can create symptoms that can be immediate or long term. These range from headaches and breathing difficulties to extreme cases of carbon monoxide poisoning that can be fatal. To prevent or reduce exposure to combustion pollution, you can:

- Install carbon monoxide detectors in your home.
- Use vented appliances whenever possible.
- Have your appliances installed by a professional.
- Test your furnace to make sure it's running properly.
- Ensure a good supply of fresh outdoor air.
- Check the venting system to be sure it is intact and is not blocked.
- Have your system inspected by a professional on a regular basis.
- Never use your stove or dryer to heat your home.

ABOVE Furniture with hard or open surfaces is easier to keep free of dust than upholstered pieces.

RIGHT Animal dander triggers allergic reactions in many people. Clean furniture and floors regularly with your vacuum's brush attachment.

Radon

Radon is the number one cause of lung cancer among non-smokers, according to EPA estimates. Radon comes from the natural (radioactive) breakdown of uranium in soil, rock, and water, and gets into the air you breathe. Radon can be found all over the United States. It can get into any type of building—homes, offices, and schools—and result in a high indoor radon level. But you and your family are most likely to get your greatest exposure at home, where you spend most of your time. Contact your local radon program representative for testing (*www.epa.gov/radon/find-information-about-local-radon-zones-and-state-contact-information*).

Outgassing

New carpeting can also have an adverse effect on indoor air. The
solvents and glues used to install carpets and their underlayment, or
padding, can contain volatile organic compounds (VOCs) that enter
the air. This is known as "outgassing." When purchasing carpet,
ask for information about the product's emissions and look for the
Carpet and Rug Institute's Green Label Plus (*www.carpet-rug.org*). If
possible, roll out and air the carpet in a well-ventilated area before
installation. Ask for low-emitting adhesives and natural backings,
and keep air flowing in the room before and after installation. You
may even consider having the carpet installed when you are not home
or are outdoors. Carpets and rugs can also trap VOCs from other

LEFT Encourage clean air inside
your home by selecting fabrics,
carpets, and furnishings that
don't outgas VOCs.

ABOVE Countertops and wall surfaces made of ceramic tile, solid-surfacing material, or plastic laminate hold up well against moisture.

materials such as paint and release them slowly over time. A healthier option is to forego wall-to-wall carpeting and use area rugs made of 100-percent organic wool, cotton, or other natural fibers. When disposing of an old carpet, check online to find a recycling service in your area.

Formaldehyde is another nasty chemical that can compromise indoor air. It may be released from particleboard cabinets, furniture, and foam insulation that contains urea-formaldehyde. New regulations under the EPA's Toxic Substances Control Act went into effect in 2018, setting limits on formaldehyde use in wood composite products. Check with the manufacturer prior to purchasing and ask about their compliance with the TSCA Title IV. When using wood products indoors, select exterior-grade wood products made with phenol-formaldehyde resin, rather than urea-formaldehyde adhesives, for floors, cabinetry, and wall finishes. If possible, choose natural materials such as solid wood, bamboo, metal, or glass.

Mold

Mold is a natural part of the environment, both outdoors and indoors. The damp conditions of many bathrooms and basements support mold growth. People with sensitivity to mold can develop allergies or respiratory irritation. You can help decrease mold levels in your home by keeping the humidity level between 40 and 60 percent. Signs that your home may not have enough airflow include stuffy-smelling air, dirty heating and cooling filters and vents, moldy storage areas, and moisture condensation on surfaces. Ventilate bathrooms, basements, kitchens, and any other area in your home that tends to be humid. Don't allow piles of boxes or other clutter to prevent proper air circulation.

A green home is healthier and more cost-effective

Pesticides

Pesticides are intended to control outbreaks of pests in agricultural fields, subduing weeds, rodents, fungi, and bacteria. But their increased use has created a wide-ranging environmental impact. Of all the natural fibers, cotton is the most heavily pesticide-laden. Water runoff from the cotton fields can pollute nearby land with chemical residues. The workers in the fields are exposed to these toxic substances while picking and packaging the cotton. Organic cotton is raised without chemical pesticides or fertilizers and is becoming much more available than ever before. Look for fabric that is organically

BELOW Using compost and organic fertilizer in flowerbeds, gardens, and lawns will help your plants thrive and reduce your exposure to toxic pesticides.

THINK GREEN

Because we spend so much time inside, indoor air pollution is a real concern. Many of these pollutants are colorless and odorless and thus go unnoticed. Awareness of the hazards can help us take positive action to improve our environment.

grown, especially in bed and bath linens that will be close to your family's skin.

Pesticides sprayed on lawns and food can affect everyone. While all ages are susceptible, the EPA feels that children are more sensitive to pesticides due to their immature immune systems, higher consumption of certain foods such as apple juice and milk, and bodily contact with the floor, animals, and lawns. The first step to reducing pesticide exposure is prevention. In your home, make sure to:

- Remove your shoes when you come inside. Not only will this help keep your home cleaner, it will reduce possible contamination of your floors and rugs with pesticides and chemicals from outdoors. This is especially important if you have small children who spend time on the floor.
- Keep food (and trash) in closed containers in your home to prevent attracting insects.
- Don't leave pet food out overnight.
- Make sure any possible site of entry for insects is sealed with screens, caulking, and weather stripping.
- Wash or vacuum floors on a regular basis.
- Keep your pets away from areas where pesticides have been applied; they are a vehicle to introduce the pesticides into your home. Before putting chemicals on your lawn, keep in mind that dogs and cats live in direct contact with the grass and lick their paws often. Likewise, avoid pesticide-laden flea collars and treatment products that come into contact with their skin and fur.
- Wash your (and your children's) hands frequently.
- If toys are dropped on the ground, clean them before you give them back to children.
- Buy clothes made from organic cotton, hemp, or other organic natural fibers.

When purchasing pesticides, the EPA suggests you read the label to find important health information before you buy. If possible, go organic when caring for your lawn and garden, and encourage your neighbors to cut down on their chemical use for the good of everyone.

Lead

Many homes built before 1978 contain lead-based paint. Lead dust can get stirred up when you scrape off old paint or replace a window. Chips of peeling paint on exterior walls mix with soil and pose a health threat, particularly to children. Kids can be exposed through normal childhood behavior, putting dirt in their mouths, and playing on the floor. If you live in an older home, you should have

the paint tested for lead content. If found, it should be removed by a professional. See the EPA's website for an up-to-date list of certified testers and renovators in your area.

Lead may also be found in household plumbing and water lines, especially in homes built before 1986. It gets into the water by corrosion of the solder in the pipes and fittings in your plumbing, as well as brass- and chrome-plated faucets and fixtures. Since 2014, stricter manufacturing regulations have decreased the amount of lead allowed in pipes, fittings, and fixtures. Your local drinking water authority can provide you with information on your home's service lines and connect you with a laboratory for testing your tap water for lead. If your home tests positive, some simple steps you can take to reduce the lead in your water are:

- Use cold water for drinking and cooking.
- Run the water before you use it, especially if it hasn't been used for more than six hours.
- Use a filter certified by NSF International to remove lead.
- Serve your family meals that are low in fat and high in calcium, iron, and vitamin C to help prevent storage of lead in the body.

ABOVE The way you choose to decorate your home should be a balance between reflecting your personal style and choosing eco-friendly materials.

25

Water

Many parts of our country have problems with both the quantity and quality of water. There are ways you can help conserve this precious resource, and the energy it takes to transport and filter it. Start by using native plant species in your landscaping that do not require a great deal of watering to maintain. Don't let the water run while you brush your teeth or shave. You can purchase a shutoff valve to attach to the showerhead, which allows you to briefly stop the water while you lather up your body or work in the shampoo. Make sure you have a full load when you run the dishwasher and laundry machine. Keep a jug of water in the refrigerator so you don't need to run the tap until it is cold. Finally, look for low-flow appliances that use less water by design.

Renewable Resources

Natural resources are potentially renewable if they are replaced at a rate equivalent to their consumption. Renewable sources of energy include wind, solar, and hydropower (water). When possible, choose products made of potentially renewable resources such as hemp, bamboo, cotton, cork, and certain types of fast-growing wood.

ABOVE Because water is an increasingly scarce commodity, reducing consumption can make a real difference.

Making Your Life More Eco-Friendly

Set priorities; review what choices are available and focus on those. There are some things you may not be able to control, such as the source of your power. Being practical makes going green possible. Make a working list of your commitments and keep track as you go along. Many changes will be easy, and you will wonder why you didn't make them sooner!

You may need to pressure the government to consider the impact of its decisions on global ecosystems and communities. To get an in-depth area pollution report, visit the website *www.scorecard.org*. By

THINK GREEN

The EPA website *www.epa.gov/kids* can introduce children of all ages to environmental issues, and provides educational resources for parents and teachers as well.

The National Institutes of Health (NIH) has an environmental health website, *www.nih.gov/health-information*, that covers many topics, including household poisons, indoor air pollution, electromagnetic fields, and environmental health.

LEFT When furnishing your home, choose natural materials like wicker, rattan, or bamboo. Not only are they comfortable and attractive, but they are also ecologically sound because they are renewable materials and often handmade.

ABOVE Rooms with an abundance of natural light are both psychologically and ecologically beneficial. Light-color rugs, window treatments, and wall coverings reflect light from outdoors.

entering your zip code, you can obtain a report on pollutants in your area. The "Take Action" page will help you get involved in your community.

Vote with your wallet for products that are environmentally friendly. When making new purchases, consider if items can be recycled or are biodegradable. Decrease your consumption and waste. Don't throw out items when it's not necessary. Think: can I reupholster, repaint, repair, refinish, or renew it?

When replacing appliances, pick energy-efficient pieces. Use cold water for laundry. Close doors and air registers in rooms not being used. This saves money in summer and winter.

Incorporate items into your daily life that minimize pollution:

- Use cloth napkins instead of paper.
- Use old cloth diapers or rags for dusting.
- Carry a reusable water bottle or hot drink thermos.
- Recycle paper products.
- Use a cloth pouch or glass container to hold your sandwich instead of wrapping it in plastic wrap or foil.
- Use a lunch box instead of a paper bag.

- If you have children or pets, use slipcovers on your furniture that can be removed and washed. This will increase the life of your furniture and lessen increasing landfills.

  Ask yourself these questions before you buy something:
- What's on the label?
- Does it have an Energy Star label?
- Is it biodegradable?
- Does it contain recycled material?
- Can I recycle it?

Look Ahead, Not Behind

History buffs like to say that you can't understand the present unless you understand the past. Take the lessons we have learned from our mistakes, and live a more natural and eco-friendly life to ensure a better future.

BELOW LEFT Plain white bone china is a classic look that goes with everything. Cloth napkins are more eco-friendly because they can be laundered and reused.

BELOW RIGHT Color is a sensual pleasure that enhances life. A simple vase of flowers gives a room a refreshing splash of color that can improve mood and stimulate the appetite.

CHAPTER 2

Decorating *Naturally*

An eco-friendly approach to home style

The decision to furnish a home with natural products is both simple and practical. Everyone feels comfortable with them. They connect you to the earth. They are products that never go out of style, and they age well. Think of the patina on an old wooden farm table or the soft feel of a pure cotton pillowcase after several washings.

TIME MAKES MOST NATURAL FURNISHINGS and fabrics even more appealing and user friendly. But just as important, they are products that are friendly to our environment as well. When you're finished with them, they won't be tossed into a landfill for countless years. They are biodegradable; they go back to the earth and leave few chemicals in their wake.

Until very recently, many products for the home were made with chemicals designed to make the manufacturing process more efficient and less costly. This emphasis on cheap, quick production has harmed our environment. Luckily, a turnaround has begun. More and more, companies are taking responsibility for the effects their products have on the earth and are working toward safer manufacturing methods. As consumers continue to ask for—and purchase—natural products, you can expect to see more on the market.

OPPOSITE This living room features a range of natural textures, weights, colors, and finishes that work beautifully together.

ABOVE The mix of textiles and patterns in the lampshades, headboard, pillows, bedding, curtains, and flooring give this master bedroom an interesting, contemporary look.

Textiles

Fabrics are often the basis around which to decorate a room. They're used for window and floor covering, upholstery, cushions, bed sheets, bath towels, and table linens. The fibers that you choose are important not only for their color and pattern, but also for the way they drape and how they wear. More natural fabrics are available today than ever before. Organic materials that are colored with natural dyes can initially be more expensive than synthetics. In the long term, however, they are a wiser investment for the health of both your family and the environment.

When you're picking out a fabric, keep in mind how you're going to use it. Your choice of fabric for a throw pillow or a much-used sofa will depend on its durability, texture, and weight. For example, sheer voile is great for delicate drapery panels, but wouldn't hold up well as a seat cushion. You may love the look of a fabric, but you should take a swatch of it home before you buy. Pull it slightly to check its resilience or fragility. Hold it up to a window to see if the weight and texture are right. Before you clean any fabric, check the manufacturer's care label.

Cotton

Cotton is made from fibers that develop around the seedpod of the cotton plant. It's a sturdy fiber that can withstand regular washings, which is why it's used for napkins, tablecloths, sheets, and towels. The length of the fiber determines the quality. Pima, Egyptian, and Supima cotton are all made with extra-long fibers that make them stronger and softer than regular cotton. A wide array of fabrics is woven from cotton; you may be familiar with batiste, organdy, percale, chintz, jacquard, duck, and corduroy.

LEFT Cotton is one of the most versatile of all natural fibers. Cotton fabrics are excellent for high-use family rooms because they can usually be machine washed.

One ecological concern is that cotton plants are often treated with fungicides, herbicides, and pesticides. The chemical residues that are used in cotton seem to dissipate after processing, but it can have a lasting effect on the environment, as well as the workers involved in growing and harvesting. Luckily, there is quite a bit of organic cotton being grown under guidelines that allow for few, if any, synthetic chemicals to be used. Organic certification refers to the field, but not the factory. Finished textiles are only guaranteed to be chemical-free in their processing if they are certified by Global Organic Textile Standards (GOTS). This certification also considers workers' rights and the environmental impact of the textiles being certified.

Some growers are crossbreeding natural self-colored cottons that do not require any dyes. They come in a range of natural earth tones—rusts, creams, browns, and greens. The colors deepen with age and become more intense the more they are washed. The cost of producing these cottons is high because production quantities are small, but they benefit the environment because they use fewer resources to produce.

Most cotton furnishings are machine washable. Before cleaning, you should check for colorfastness and shrinkage. If you're unsure about how much it will shrink, wash it at a low temperature. Cotton slipcovers should be washed on a gentle cycle and dried flat to maintain their shape. Iron cotton furnishings with a hot iron while they are slightly damp.

Muslin

Muslin is plain, finely woven cotton that varies in weight. Available as bleached or unbleached, some varieties are used for sheeting and lightweight curtains; heavier weights are generally used for slipcovers. Muslin imparts a casual, lived-in feel to contemporary or country interiors.

Canvas

Canvas is a plain cotton fabric with a coarse weave. Its strength and durability make canvas useful for a wide variety of purposes: sails, tents, and as a surface for oil paintings, just to name a few. Canvas is a good, low-cost choice for casual upholstery that must withstand plenty of wear and tear.

Both canvas and muslin can be washed with mild soap in cold water. Avoid putting either material in a hot dryer, as they can shrink.

Hemp

Hemp is one of nature's sturdiest and longest-lasting materials. It comes from a type of plant that is specially bred to yield long fibers. Because the robust hemp plant requires very little water and grows well without pesticides or herbicides, it's considered an eco-friendly fiber. Traditionally, hemp's coarseness made it most useful for heavy-duty applications, such as rope. However, advances in manufacturing have made hemp softer and more adaptable for clothing and home furnishings. Today's hemp fabrics accept dye more readily than cotton or linen, and they are now manufactured in a wide variety of colors.

Wash hemp in cold water with similar colors; tumble dry on low heat. Never use bleach, and remove from the dryer as soon as possible; shake to remove any wrinkles.

Linen

Linen is made from the fibers of the flax plant. It has a tailored, crisp feel and is one of the more durable fibers available. Because the fibers are also very absorbent, linen is often used for towels and tablecloths. One of linen's most beautiful characteristics is its texture, a slightly uneven feel and appearance that marks it as a natural fiber. Linen has a beautiful range of subtle shades, from cream to dark tan to gray.

ABOVE The neutral tone of this natural-canvas sofa provides the backdrop for fabrics in bright colors and patterns.

ABOVE This master bedroom is a good example of how several patterns can combine harmoniously. The striped wall covering, rattan headboard, checked bedspread, and printed bedskirt work beautifully together because of their shared central color theme.

Slight shrinkage is possible when it's washed, so it's often preshrunk. As we all know, linen does wrinkle easily, but to many, this is part of its charm. Linen sheets are popular for bedding because they are cool, absorbent, and wonderful against the skin. Opt for GOTS-certified, organically grown linen if it's available, because some fabrics may have been treated with pesticides.

Although linen is a strong fiber, it's best to launder it as gently as possible. Don't wash it in a temperature above 80 degrees Fahrenheit (25 degrees Celsius), and avoid using bleach. Instead, wash linen with mild soap in warm water and avoid the dryer. Thinner fabrics, such as those used in curtains, should be washed using the gentle washing cycle with a large quantity of water. Iron on the wrong side while the fabric is still damp to prevent an unattractive sheen. For napkins, tablecloths, and sheets, try folding at different places each time before storing. Constant creasing tends to show permanent fold marks over time.

Ramie

Ramie is harvested from the woody stems of nettle plants indigenous to Asia. A strong natural fiber, it has an unusual resistance to bacteria and mold. Ramie is lustrous, holds its shape well, and is often used in blends.

Like linen and other textiles made from wood fibers, ramie should be given special care during cleaning. It should be hand or machine washed on a gentle cycle in cold water. Do not put ramie in a dryer; instead, lay it flat to air dry. Ramie should not be sharply folded when storing.

Silk

For centuries, silk has been prized as a luxurious fabric. It comes from the cocoon of the silk worm and is expensive to produce. The fiber is woven into a variety of fabrics, from delicate crepe de chine to rough-textured raw silk. Silk takes dye well and is available in a dazzling array of colors. It's soft and resilient, but does require some coddling, so it would be more appropriate for accent pillows or a bedcover

BELOW Richly colored fabrics and a few favorite beach mementos on a bedside table guarantee sweet dreams.

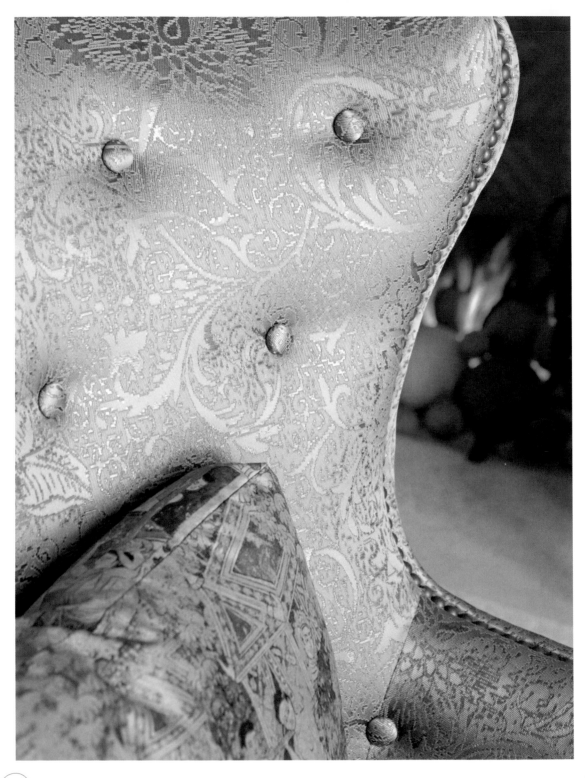

rather than a well-used sofa in the family room. Avoid exposure to sunlight.

Dry-cleaning is often recommended, especially for fabrics with more than one color, lined window treatments, or intricately sewn pillows. However, in an eco-friendly home, you might want to seek another method. Some silk items can be washed, but a few precautions should be taken first. If there are any items glued to the surface, such as sequins, appliqués, or rhinestones, don't wash the piece. You should test a hidden area, such as a hem, to make sure the dyes are colorfast. If you've checked it thoroughly, you can proceed to hand wash it using cold water and a mild soap.

Wool

Wool is fabric woven from the fleece of sheep and other animals. It's heavier and longer lasting than most other natural fibers, so it's often used in carpets, rugs, cushion covers, and throws. One special advantage of sheep's wool is that it is naturally fire resistant and can be used to make bedding and sleepwear, which by law are required to be fireproof and contain potentially harmful fire-retardant chemicals. Because wool fibers have the ability to bounce back to their natural shape when stretched, wool is a good choice for upholstery fabric or rugs that get a lot of foot traffic.

Look for organic wool products with the GOTS-certified label. This means that the animals (sheep, goats, alpaca, rabbits, etc.) have been raised with sustainable, humane ranching practices, including pesticide-free pastures and chemical-free animal feed. It also ensures ecological and socially responsible practices along the entire production chain, including natural dyes and no chemical mothproofing added. Avoid moth damage by storing wool items with herbal moth bags or cedar chips.

Wool is fairly stain resistant because of the lanolin in the fibers. If something spills, blot it as soon as possible with a paper or cloth

ABOVE Small details, such as these delicately fringed and beaded silk pillows, add luxury to any decorating scheme.

OPPOSITE Silk brocade is a decadent, but natural, choice for this chair cover, sure to become the room's focal point.

THINK GREEN

Eco-Options for Dry-Cleaning

Many fabrics are labeled "dry-clean only" by manufacturers. For many years, dry cleaners in the United States have relied on perchloroethylene (often called PERC) as the solvent used during the dry-cleaning process. Recently, concerns about the health risks and environmental effects of PERC have promoted the development of more eco-friendly cleaning processes, such as wet cleaning and CO_2 cleaning, which is endorsed by the EPA Design for the Environment Program.

If you must have something dry-cleaned, refuse to accept items that have a strong chemical smell, which indicates that too much PERC was used in the cleaning process. Air-dry furnishings before using them to get rid of any solvent fumes.

Wet-cleaning: Professional wet-cleaning is the most commercially available, nontoxic alternative to dry-cleaning. Its water-based, energy-efficient technology uses computer-controlled washers and dryers and specially formulated biodegradable detergents and finishing equipment to process garments that have the dry-cleaning label. Wet-cleaning is comparable to dry-cleaning in quality and price.

CO_2 cleaning: CO_2 is a nontoxic, odorless, naturally occurring gas that's a byproduct of existing industrial processes. When subjected to pressure, it becomes a liquid solvent. When liquid CO_2 is injected into a washing chamber, it dissolves fats, oils, and dirt. The process produces no hazardous wastes or emissions.

BELOW Breathable and soft, wool and cotton make ideal fabrics for a comfy bed that may be too inviting to resist.

towel. Because wool usually can't be washed, dry-cleaning is recommended for a more thorough cleansing. Upholstery or window treatments should be vacuumed regularly with a brush attachment to remove surface dirt.

Where You Sleep

A good place to begin using natural materials is in the bedroom. About one third of your life is spent in bed, so it makes sense that you make it as eco-friendly as possible. Because your body regenerates from the stresses of the day while you're asleep, making this space a healthy haven is of utmost importance.

A good bed is the most important part of the bedroom. Most mattresses are made with polyurethane foam, sprayed with fire retardants, and covered with polyester plastic fabric. On top, mattresses and mattress pads can be made of synthetic materials and treated with water- and stain-repellant chemicals. When you sleep, you inhale whatever is in these materials, including dust mites, mold

ABOVE LEFT A natural linen sofa and bold throw pillows balance beautifully with the dramatic black baby-grand piano.

ABOVE RIGHT The quiet interplay of velvet, silk, and satin in low-key, natural colors whispers luxury in this master suite.

41

ABOVE When choosing materials for your bedroom, look for natural fibers, organic cottons, solid-wood furniture, and chemical-free mattresses.

from moisture-trapping synthetic mattresses, and toxic chemicals released by fire retardants, glues, fabric treatments, dyes, and pesticide residues in conventional wool and cotton battings.

It is definitely worth seeking out a mattress that is made of organic cotton or wool so you won't be sleeping on—or breathing in—harmful chemicals. For the mattress core, look for natural latex, a sustainable product derived from the rubber tree. Only the GOTS or Global Organic Latex Standards (GOLS) certification ensures that you are buying a mattress made without harmful chemicals. A lower-price option is a mattress stuffed with a mix of natural and synthetic latex—it's not perfect, but better than polyurethane foam. If you're not ready to swap your conventional mattress for an organic one, natural, rubber-latex mattress pads, organic wool toppers, or tightly woven mattress casings are widely available options that will deliver a more comfortable and healthful sleep.

No matter how eco-friendly you want to be, the most important thing to look for in a mattress is comfort. Figure out what size is best for you and what your bedroom dimensions will allow. After that, feel it, lie on it, and see whether you like the firmness of the mattress. In the end, it's a personal choice. But if you share the bed with someone, take him or her along while you're shopping. Whether you're a back sleeper or a side sleeper, get in your normal position and see whether the mattress is right for you.

Bed frames come in many shapes and sizes. It's important that the bed is sturdy and well made so it withstands weight and stress without creaking or bowing. Find a frame constructed of a solid, strong natural material like wood, bamboo, or metal. Avoid veneers, particleboard, or laminates that might contain toxic chemicals. Another green solution is to buy a bed made from salvaged wood, or choose a vintage model from an antique store.

LEFT Chemical-free wool or organic cotton bed coverings are the gold standard for an eco-friendly bedroom.

Pillow Talk

Eco-friendly pillows can be filled with buckwheat, natural latex, kapok, hemp, pure wool, or organic cotton. Buckwheat pillows are popular in Asia, where they have been used for thousands of years. Many people like them for the way they conform to the body, a quality that can soothe neck pain. Kapok is a fiber from the seedpod of the tropical kapok tree. It has a similar feel to goose down. Wool is a good material because it is soft and absorbent. Whatever you choose, look for an outer casing made of soft, organic cotton, or sateen.

Organic pillow fillings range from buckwheat to wool

Linens

Linen options for the bed are just as numerous. While organic cotton and linen are popular for their cool, crisp feel, there are alternative fibers, such as hemp, that are sustainable and produced without chemicals, pesticides, or herbicides. Fabrics marketed as bamboo or

LIVE WISE, LIVE WELL

Although they cost a bit more up front, front-load and advanced top-load washers that earn the Energy Star label can save 6 gallons of water per load. Without agitators, they flip and spin clothes in a reduced stream of water. They save energy and are gentler on fabrics, too. High Efficiency (HE) labels alone are not indicators of energy efficiency; they simply correspond to HE low-sudsing detergents. Look for the Energy Star certification on washers and dryers, which use 25% less energy and 33% less water than standard washers.

wood pulp may actually be rayon, which is heavily processed and not a very sustainable or eco-friendly option. Be sure to check the fabric care label before you purchase an alternative fiber because some of them hold up better than others in the washer and dryer. When laundering your all-natural bedding, avoid harsh chemicals. Look for gentle, biodegradable detergents. Wash them in cold water and hang dry.

Blankets

There are many natural fiber choices available for blankets, and all are luxuriously soft. Alpaca wool is silky and warmer than sheep's wool. Cashmere is a luxury fabric that is lightweight, yet warm, while woven organic cotton makes a lightweight blanket.

Comforting Colors

Whites or neutrals create a restful, soothing ambiance in the bedroom that encourages sweet dreams. If you'd like some color, choose the palest shades of blue, green, or pink.

RIGHT Muted tones picked up by several fabrics in this quiet room set the mood for a good night's sleep.

Floor Coverings

The terms "carpet" and "rug" are often used interchangeably, but they're not the same. Carpeting is manufactured in rolls ranging from just over 2 feet (0.5 meters) wide to broadlooms that measure as much as 18 feet (5.5 meters) wide. Carpeting is usually laid wall to wall and can be installed over raw subflooring, although it is usually installed over a pad. Rugs don't extend wall to wall and are used over another finished flooring surface.

Carpeting

There are advantages to wall-to-wall carpeting. It adds softness and warmth to a room, both visually and physically. Carpeting also muffles room noise and reduces the amount of sound that is transmitted to rooms on lower floors of the house. It's easy to maintain if you have a good vacuum cleaner and can cover floors that are of poor, uneven quality. However, there are many concerns about the negative impact of carpeting on the environment as well

ABOVE Carpeting can add comfort and beautiful texture to a room. Wool fibers or recycled materials are the best eco-friendly choices.

as your own indoor air quality. Synthetic and treated natural carpets emit hazardous chemicals and are not biodegradable when tossed in landfills. Carpets harbor particulates as well as dust mites and, if not meticulously cleaned, can also be a problem for those with allergies or asthma. Many carpets have adhesives and backings that contain unhealthy chemicals.

It is possible to find wall-to-wall carpeting that has much less impact on your home and the environment. Look for 100-percent pure wool without dyes, stain guards, or other chemicals. Recyclable carpet tiles made from corn-based fibers are also available. Wall-to-wall carpeting made from recycled PET plastic bottles is another ingenious alternative. Additional eco-friendly options include felt underlay made from recycled fabrics or chemical-free jute and hemp. When buying a carpet, choose products that are certified as safe by the Carpet and Rug Institute (CRI).

Area Rugs

BELOW An area rug is a good option for the busy entryway of a home. It can be cleaned easily and repositioned if portions begin to show wear or stains. To keep the rug in place, use a nonslip felt pad underneath.

Another way to enjoy warmth and softness underfoot without actually laying wall-to-wall carpeting is to buy area rugs. These are great for highlighting a beautiful hardwood, stone, or ceramic tile floor or to define space in a room. Area rugs can add an instant shot of color and pattern to an otherwise neutral color scheme. Their

portability is an asset because they can be removed for easy cleaning or a change of seasons. And if you move, you can take the rug with you—a truly eco-friendly alternative.

Wool

Wool is an ideal fabric for floor coverings because it's soft, durable, and holds dyes well. For centuries, many cultures around the globe have developed trademark woven designs. For example, Oriental rugs have long been treasured for their beautiful patterns and their ability to harmonize with a variety of styles. Because wool carpets are so durable, there are many opportunities to find a secondhand or vintage item in excellent condition. Wool throw rugs can be found at antique fairs and flea markets in styles and colors that go well with many of today's decorating schemes. If you want something new, look for organic wool made from plant and animal yarns that are pesticide free. Try to find a carpet that has natural dyes.

Cotton

Cotton rugs, such as Turkish kilims or dhurries from India, are a lighter alternative to wool coverings. They are not as durable or long lasting, but make a fine warm-weather replacement for heavy winter rugs. Bathrooms are a great place for cotton rugs because they can absorb spills and splashes and simply line dry. If the size isn't too large, your cotton rug can be washed in cool water and thrown into a clothes dryer on a low setting.

Other Natural Fibers

Apart from wool and cotton, natural fibers such as jute, sisal, hemp, coir, and sea grass have been used as floor covers for centuries. These materials are usually biodegradable and are manufactured without harmful chemicals. Their neutral tones and natural variations in both color and texture make a perfect fit for natural interiors. Fibers may vary in terms of durability and stain resistance, so ask about their merits and limitations before purchasing. Some are best used with padding underneath to prevent them from slipping.

Because they are made from plant fiber, they are very absorbent. Exposure to the elements or extreme changes in humidity levels can make them subject to mold or mildew. This means that most should be kept from areas like basements, bathrooms, kitchens, and porches where dampness or spills are likely to occur. For regular maintenance,

ABOVE The carpet in this room ties together all the colors used in the furniture, pillows, and window treatments.

it's best to vacuum often, not wash or shampoo them. If a spill does occur, blot it—never rub—with an absorbent white towel.

SEA GRASS

Grown in China, sea grass has a soft, silky texture when woven that's smoother than some of the other natural fibers. Generally light brown or beige with tinges of green, sea grass rugs enhance many contemporary color schemes. Although sea grass is stain-resistant, prolonged exposure to water can cause damage, so avoid using it in a bathroom. Don't install sea grass on stairs because it has a tendency to be slippery.

HEMP

Hemp is made from a plant in the cannabis family and is used for a growing range of home products. It's extremely durable and, while more expensive than some other natural fibers, will last for years with proper care. Since it uses much less water to grow than cotton does, it's also gentler on the planet.

JUTE

Jute is made from the fibrous inner bark of a large herbaceous plant that grows in hot, damp regions of Asia. It is processed into burlap bags, rug backings, and rope. Because they feel soft underfoot, jute rugs are ideal for bedroom floors. However, jute is not practical for areas of heavy wear because it is harder to clean than other natural fibers and can develop watermarks if it gets wet. The edges of a jute rug should be hemmed with a canvas border to prevent fraying.

SISAL

Sisal has traditionally been used in the production of rope and twine. It comes from the leaves of the agave plant. Because sisal fibers are tough, it doesn't compress and show wear patterns. Sisal can be woven with other fibers, such as wool, to create a product that combines the softness of wool and the durability of sisal. One caveat, however: sisal has a coarse texture and shouldn't be used in areas where young children or pets spend time on the floor.

COIR

Coir, or coco fiber, is processed from the outer husk of a coconut shell. This material is softened and woven to produce sturdy mats. You've probably seen coir used as a door mat, but it can be used indoors as well. It is resistant to water, sunlight, and insects, making it a good choice near a backyard pool. Flip the mat periodically to keep the edges from curling.

BELOW This natural-fiber rug defines the living area in a large room and emphasizes the natural beauty of the wood floor.

Natural Furniture

Furniture has three basic functions in the home: seating, sleeping, and storage. It provides a cozy sitting area as well as a place for entertaining. Perhaps you may need a furniture arrangement to define living and dining areas within a single room. In a natural-style home, your furniture must reflect your personal taste, fulfill a practical function, and be constructed of organic materials.

Solid wood is the material of choice for a natural-style home. It's durable, ages well, and has tones and textures that harmonize with other natural materials and colors. As it ages, wood acquires a beautiful patina that can't be artificially duplicated. Furniture can be constructed of hardwood or softwood. Hardwoods are from deciduous trees such as cherry, maple, oak, pecan, teak, mahogany, and poplar. Hardwoods are often used in high-quality furniture because they are stronger than softwoods. Softwoods come from conifer trees such as fir, pine, redwood, cedar, and cypress. They are kiln dried and well seasoned before use to prevent splitting and splintering. A wood surface can always be sanded and refinished if cracks or stains appear on the surface, while veneers can be hard to replace. Treat wood with care, dusting and lightly waxing it regularly. Wipe off water stains as quickly as you can to avoid unsightly rings.

Sofas and other upholstered pieces are a little trickier to shop for because it's sometimes hard to tell exactly what you're getting from looks alone. The term "solid wood" means that the exposed surfaces are made of natural wood without added veneer or plywood. Solid hardwood is the strongest—and most costly—furniture option. A more economical, eco-friendly furniture choice is a veneer of decorative wood on top of a layer of an abundant wood species.

When selecting a sofa, check it out carefully before buying. After all, it's an investment that you want to last for many years. Sit on it, lean back, and look underneath to study how it's constructed. Choose solid wood or plywood covered with melamine or veneers. It should be fabricated with strong dovetail joints, rather than staples and glue. Ask the retailer how much synthetic material was used in construction, especially what type of filling, glues, or varnish were

THINK GREEN

Eco Tips for Choosing Furniture

The Forest Stewardship Council (FSC) is an international organization that brings together representatives of human rights and environmental organizations, the forest industry, and timber users to find solutions to the problems created by bad forestry practices and to reward good forest management. Members include furniture companies and nonprofit organizations such as Greenpeace and the Sierra Club. When buying wood products, look for the FSC label, which assures you that the wood was grown and harvested in a sustainable manner.

Look into products made with lesser-known species of wood such as sweet gum or California Oak or FSC-certified woods, such as teak, mahogany, ipe, or rubberwood. Avoid tropical or exotic hardwoods like zebrawood and ebony. In addition, many companies now use wood products from farms that raise trees solely for lumber so that no forests are destroyed. Trust the FSC certification more than the type of wood. The same species of tree may be sustainably logged in one country but illegal and endangered in another.

- Reclaimed wood: Many designers and furniture manufacturers are making use of the wood that's already out there and using this reclaimed wood to make furniture. Some companies buy reclaimed lumber and cut it to specifications. Others rework salvaged wood from old furniture, houses, and factory scraps into new wood furniture. Wherever it comes from, it is an efficient way to reuse a resource.

- Recycled metal and plastic: Plastics and metals may not fit into the natural category, but they do get an eco-friendly thumbs up when designers recycle them to make furniture. Fewer natural resources are wasted, and materials that would otherwise end up in a landfill are repurposed into attractive and useful pieces.

BELOW The strong weave of a sisal carpet is able to withstand the weight of heavy furniture.

THINK GREEN

Organic Cleaners

- Wood furniture cleaner: Mix 1 tsp. olive oil with 1 cup (230 milliliters) white vinegar. Dip a soft rag into the solution, and wipe lightly over furniture to dust and polish.

- Glass cleaner: Mix 2 tsp. distilled white vinegar with one quart (940 milliliters) water. Spritz on a soft, lint-free cloth, and wipe on windows.

- Copper and brass cleaner: Mix salt and vinegar to make a paste. Wipe on surface with a soft rag, and rub clean.

- Silver polish: Make a paste of baking soda and water. Rub onto item with a wet sponge, rinse in hot water, and dry with a soft cloth.

RIGHT Simple and elegant, wood furniture has a timeless beauty that appeals to everyone.

used in the product. Many manufacturers are offering eco-friendly cushion filling made from soy-based foam or natural rubber latex; others are using recycled wire and steel coils. When selecting fabric, choose eco-friendly hemp, organic cotton, or linen.

Bamboo

Bamboo is becoming the go-to material for many products in the home, including furniture, floors, and countertops. The durability and short growing time make it a realistic, attractive, and sturdy alternative to traditional wood.

Other Materials

Wicker, rattan, cane, and rush also add warmth and texture that are perfect complements to the muted colors and simple lines of natural interiors. What you would normally think of as garden furniture— twig tables, Adirondack chairs, and even metal café tables—evoke the feel of the outdoors in the living room.

ABOVE LEFT This unusual chair and table is handmade from ecologically friendly materials.

ABOVE RIGHT Bamboo and rattan furniture looks just as at home in an interior setting as on the patio.

What's Old Is New

Some good sources for furniture made of natural materials are flea markets, antique stores, or salvage yards. There you can find vintage wood pieces that have developed a fine patina of age and historical charm. Old oak tables, Shaker chairs with rush seats, and solid-maple dressers have the simple lines and rich textures that go well with natural décor. The Internet offers hundreds of sites that sell vintage pieces at reasonable prices. One added benefit is that quality vintage furniture usually has excellent resale value.

When shopping for vintage pieces, follow the same rules of thumb that you would use for any furniture purchase. Make sure the piece is solidly built with no loose or broken joints and has no mold, mildew, or dry rot. Take a measuring tape with you to make sure the piece fits the area you want to fill. Nothing is quite as annoying as purchasing furniture only to discover that you can't get it through the front door or that it's too big for the living room.

Look around your house. There's nothing more eco-friendly than repurposing an old piece of furniture that has outgrown its original duty. Using an old bench in your bathroom or a bedroom dresser as an extra cabinet in the kitchen not only gives you low-cost storage, but also adds an eclectic and personal character that is the essence of natural style. Refinishing old but well-built furniture can be costly, but ultimately you'll get a piece that you can use for many years.

You can slipcover or reupholster a solidly constructed sofa or chair. Slipcovers are usually a less expensive option. The look is more casual and often well suited to the design of a natural home. Another benefit is that slipcovers can be removed and easily washed at home. Unless you're experienced, leave reupholstering to a professional. Finding an upholsterer or furniture restorer is best done by word of mouth. Ask friends and acquaintances whose taste you admire for references. Make sure you discuss with the upholsterer exactly what you want, and get an estimate beforehand. You can buy your own eco-friendly fabric and choose what kind of fillings you would like to use in the piece. A talented upholsterer can change the look of your furniture in subtle ways. They can add a skirt, cording, or pleats. When ordering fabric, remember to include extra material for coordinating throw pillows.

Ultimately, the furniture you decide to purchase shouldn't look trendy. Buy quality pieces with classic lines and natural fibers that will last a lifetime. Remember, the new furniture that you buy today may become a treasure for the next generation to enjoy.

LEFT Furnishing your house with antiques or flea-market finds is not only eco-friendly, but also gives your home a richness of texture and patina that can't be found in new furniture.

OPPOSITE An antique clock makes a stunning focal point in any room.

Bring Nature into Your Home

The most natural home is one that reflects you and what you love. There are endless ways to make nature an important part of your decorating scheme. Take a walk outside and see what most inspires you, then bring it into your home. It will make your home a sanctuary from the rigors and stresses of the mechanized and stressful world outside your door.

Flowers, Foliage, and Plants

A vase of fresh flowers is an instant link with the outdoors. The good thing is that you don't need dozens to make an impact. One brilliantly colored bloom in a bud vase can light up a desk or a kitchen counter. Although you can buy practically any kind of fresh flowers all year round from a florist, you'll find them at their best when they're in season and local. An added bonus: flowers bought during their natural growing period are often cheaper. Floral arrangements shouldn't be stiff; they should be loose and unstructured like the

BELOW Flowering houseplants bring color, texture, and the sweet smells of nature into a room.

THINK GREEN

Save on summer cooling costs by installing a trellis for vines on your south-facing exterior wall. Jasmine, grape, and ivy are popular choices. The vines will absorb and reflect the sun's energy in the summer. In the winter, the energy will reach the wall or window and warm the surface. Vines will also help to reduce noise and dust.

LEFT Herbs such as chives, dill, and basil are easy to grow in a sunny kitchen window and give you a perennial supply for cooking.

ABOVE When choosing houseplants, consider the amount of light and the temperature of the room.

flowers grown in a field or a country garden. Twigs, branches, pinecones, ivy, and berries are easy to find and add a sculptural feel to a floral display. Dried flowers and seedpods make lush arrangements that can be just as beautiful but longer lasting than their fresh counterparts. Dried hydrangeas massed together in a vase have a soft hue and lush texture that will bring back memories of summer.

Don't overlook foliage for natural displays. Leaves from oak trees or leafy ferns look beautiful when clipped together and framed between two pieces of glass. Simple birch branches placed in a terra-cotta pitcher make an easy, yet striking, arrangement.

Use containers that fit with your natural theme. Look around your house, and choose objects that might not be used as a conventional vase. Flowers can be put in a glass jar filled with water and slipped inside a basket or a carved wooden box. A watering can brought in from the garden is another whimsical alternative.

Houseplants are also a must. Not only do they link us with the outdoors, but they also help improve indoor air. Plants look lush if they are grouped together and placed on a metal tray or on a wooden shelf near a sunny window. Arrange them according to size, texture, and color.

Vegetables and Fruits

Fruits and vegetables are a simple way to add seasonal color to your home with just a trip to the grocery store. A shallow bowl of lemons or limes centered on a coffee table or sideboard brings instant natural color and texture into your home. Fruits and vegetables, such as artichokes, pomegranates, gourds, or eggplants, make beautiful displays that are equal to any flower arrangement. Find other creative ways to use fruit; apples or oranges can be hollowed out and used as holders for tea lights. Not only are they colorful, but the aroma of fruit will be a sensual delight.

LIVE WISE, LIVE WELL

Plants that Clean the Air

Not only do plants enhance our décor, but they also act to control one of the biggest household problems: air pollution. Plants function as natural air filters, replacing carbon dioxide with oxygen and absorbing harmful pollutants. It has been reported that flowering plants like the gerbera daisy and chrysanthemums are beneficial in removing benzene (found in paints, inks, oils, plastics, and dyes). Philodendron and spider plants are effective in removing formaldehyde molecules found in pressed wood products, carpets, fabrics, floor coverings, and fire retardants. Other plants found to be effective in clearing the air include English ivy, bamboo palm, mother-in-law tongue, corn plant, and *Dracaena marginata*. In general, one large plant per 100 square feet (30 square meters) will effectively clean the air in an average home.

LEFT Lemons and apples make a simple yet striking centerpiece in this breakfast nook.

RIGHT An artful arrangement of old cigar boxes, drawing tools, and paintbrushes line the shelves above this weathered antique drafting table.

Found Art

A walk in the woods or a stroll down the beach are perfect opportunities to gather small treasures that will add a personal touch to your home. Souvenirs from nature let you get in sync with the seasons and offer an endless bounty of textures and colors. Pieces of driftwood or branches can be hung as artwork on a wall, electrified and used as bases for lamps, and even shaped into curtain rods. After a good scrubbing, shells can be repurposed as delicate tea light holders or soap dishes for the bathroom or kitchen. Rocks picked up from a riverbank or the local gardening center can function as

Express your nature by decorating your home with what you love

paperweights, doorstops, or plant markers in the garden. You don't have to make elaborate arrangements—the more casual, the better. They provide an emotional connection with the outdoors each time you recall the day you discovered your treasure.

Wall Art

A digital camera offers you the opportunity to bring visual memories of your time spent outside to your walls. Take a series of photos in a garden, beach, or your favorite backyard retreat. Choose various times of the day or different seasons. The subject matter doesn't have to be something fantastic—make a study of a tree in the front yard in the spring when the buds are in bloom, in summer when the leaves are green and lush, in autumn when the leaves turn ruddy,

BELOW A whimsical mix of small paintings, stacked china, and vintage planters enlivens this funky kitchen.

and in winter when the branches are sculptural and bare. Put them in matching frames and group them together in the front hallway or on the stairwell. A simple photograph of a flower can be manipulated on a color printer to make a larger-than-life print. Focus on just the blossom or include the whole stem and flower. Smaller images can be laminated for placemats, and larger images framed to occupy an entire wall.

Botanical prints are another inexpensive way to bring in the outdoors. Comb through used bookstores for vintage nature books containing pictures of insects, birds, and flowers. All make pleasing subjects to frame and hang on the wall. Even pretty notecards adorned with flowers can be framed to decorate a small area in the bathroom or bedroom.

BELOW Although similar in color, it's the contrast in textures that make this display so compelling. The puffy softness of the cotton balls, the dotted surfaces of the sea urchin shells, and the seaworn smoothness of the conch shell create a lively natural arrangement.

Containers

Hand-woven baskets made from natural fibers, such as cane and rattan, are decorative as well as useful. They make wonderful containers for fruits and vegetables, magazines, or balls of yarn, and can be indispensable for disguising everyday clutter. Baskets with lids can double as laundry hampers, trash receptacles, and even side tables. Whatever their use, they add textured warmth to your home.

LEFT A simple arrangement of calla lilies in a glass vase and a bowl heaped with fragrant lemons make excellent decorations using natural objects.

Glass is a versatile accent with reflective qualities that make it special. Put a collection of recycled glass bottles in a window and watch how their shape and color change with the light throughout the day. A vase or platter makes a perfect display container for seashore finds, pieces of ribbon, raffia, or dappled stones. Chunky vessels made from recycled glass can double as vases or candleholders. Scout flea markets and tag sales for used but still good bowls and bottles.

CHAPTER 3

The Colors of
Nature

Developing your color consciousness

Whether you choose key lime, sky blue, or sunflower yellow—or all of the above—color can be one of the most effective and easiest ways to add character and personality to your home. Color sets the tone and the mood you desire. Whether it's soothing, calm, vibrant, or cozy, rely on Mother Nature's palette for inspiration.

MANY PEOPLE FIND THAT SELECTING a color scheme is confusing because of the enormity of choices available in paints, wall coverings, fabrics, and flooring. Finding the right combination can feel overwhelming, and the fear of making a mistake leads to choosing the safe—if uninspired—choice again and again. Instead, why not look to the natural world for guidance? There, you'll find an unlimited variety of color combinations that form perfect palettes. Just remember, there are no set rules, only guidelines. Don't worry about trends. Color is an emotional and personal choice. Select the colors that inspire you and make you feel comfortable. Ultimately, these will be the ones that will feel right in your home.

OPPOSITE A pottery bowl filled with fresh limes and an informal arrangement of handpicked blooms reflect the casual, colorful style of this home.

Color Relationships

Although most people can sense whether a color pairing looks wrong or right, understanding why you feel that way can be a bit more complicated. One way to learn the how and why of color relationships is to study them on a color wheel (see page 69).

In nature, light reflected through a prism creates a rainbow of colors known as the color spectrum. The color wheel presents these hues in the form of a circle. Each band of color blends into the next, from red to violet to purple and so on. The wheel includes primary, secondary, and tertiary colors. The primaries are red, blue, and yellow. Secondary colors (green, orange, and violet) are made by combining two primary colors; tertiary colors are created when a primary color is mixed with a secondary color. For example, mixing the primary color blue with the secondary color green creates the tertiary color turquoise.

Additional color relationships include analogous color schemes, which use three colors that sit next to one another on the color wheel. These colors are harmonious because they are related. Complements appear opposite one another on the color wheel—red and green, or purple and yellow, for example. This readymade, harmonious pairing of a warm hue with a cool hue results in a high-contrast, high-energy color scheme. A split complementary scheme uses several analogous hues that are "split" from a key color (red-purple and red-orange, for example), paired with a complementary color (green) for contrast. A triadic color scheme results when any three colors are equally spaced around the color wheel. Such a trio makes a bold, vibrant color scheme. Finally, a tetradic color scheme uses four colors arranged into two complementary pairs. A four-color scheme works best when one color is dominant and attention is paid to creating a balance between warm and cool hues.

Understanding Color Temperatures

In nature, you need only to look at a cloudless sky or the ocean to understand the meaning of a cool color; observe the sun at dusk or the glow of a fire to appreciate warm colors. You can observe a range of color temperatures using the color wheel as your guide. Cool and warm color ranges appear on opposite sides of the wheel. Note that colors appear to change in their proximity to other colors. For example, a neutral green can appear warm against a cool purple or cool against a warm orange. This same green appears more intense when it is placed next to red and less intense when paired

BELOW Before making any color decisions, think about what colors inspire you, energize you, or make you feel the most serene and relaxed.

with brown. Red's and blue's intensities can be toned down to rose and sage.

Nature's Palette

The advantage of using nature as your guide to decorating your home is that it gives you thousands of examples. All you have to do it take a walk in the park. Start noticing the colors that surround you every day. Examine the flowers, the bark on the trees, the birds, or the pebbles on the ground. Study how all of nature's colors interact with each other. Although many of these colors may be bright, they have the right proportion, value, and intensity to be harmonious. Observe how the sun reflects on the grass in the early morning or after a rain to see how the same colors intensify with moisture. Go when it's misty

CLOCKWISE FROM TOP LEFT The illustrations below show the basic color wheel and examples of classic color pairings, including analogous (red, red-orange, and orange-yellow); triadic (purple, red, and yellow); tetradic (purple, red, yellow, and green); split complementary (orange-yellow, yellow-green, and purple); and complementary (red and green).

Basic Color Wheel

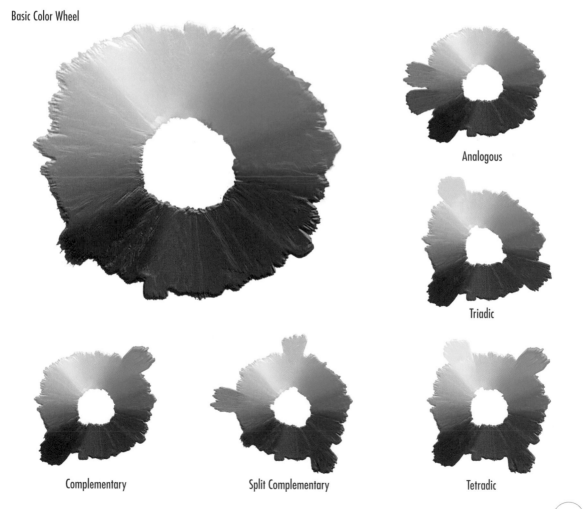

Analogous

Triadic

Complementary

Split Complementary

Tetradic

ABOVE The warm neutrals in this room are punctuated with bright yellow and turquoise to create a richer, more interesting effect.

and see how the colors look quiet, yet balanced. Examine how nature combines color: the yellow and brown in a sunflower, the subtle variations in the bark of a tree, the nuances of white in a seashell. Notice the changes of color throughout the seasons. Spring's hues are fresh greens or gentle yellows that change to darker greens and lavenders with the intense sun of summer. Autumn gives us browns, rusts, and oranges, while winter brings more neutral shades of taupe and gray. The next time you're in the produce aisle, study the different shades and tones of the fruits and vegetables. All these things can serve as a starting point for developing harmonious color schemes, textures, and patterns.

Color Consciousness

Most people can say they have a favorite color. It may be the memory of a favorite childhood dress or the color of a first bike. This color preference is often linked to a person, place, or experience that makes you happy and imparts a sense of well-being. Different hues have been shown to affect your mood. How would you like to feel? Use your favorite colors to evoke the mood you want.

Earth Tones: Colors from Nature

Green is a comfortable, healing color. Nature's ultimate neutral hue, it is found everywhere in many warm and cool shades. These can be as vibrant as lime, as intense as newly mowed grass, or as subtle as moss on the side of a rock. Green symbolizes freshness and new growth. Because of its soothing qualities, it is often used to encourage relaxation, such as in a hospital waiting room or a spa. Practically every color will blend with some shade of green. Red, yellow, orange, blue, and violet all make intriguing accents. Celadon, pistachio, and khaki are chic colors that create serene environments, especially when mixed together in subtly varying shades.

THINK GREEN

Smarter Painting

Turpentine, paint thinner, and other paintbrush cleaners are toxic and can pollute water, so use them with caution. That means plenty of ventilation, avoiding skin contact, and wearing safety glasses. Once used, pour the dirty solvent into a labeled glass jar. Within a week or two, the solid dirt in the solvent will fall to the bottom of the jar. Pour the remaining clean solvent into its original container for future use. Dispose of the solids properly. Save the jar to repeat the process.

LEFT Nature's color combinations are the perfect starting point to explore our own color preferences.

RIGHT The many shades of green in this bedroom add a tranquil feel and pair up beautifully with blue.

Blue denotes loyalty, integrity, and honesty. It's also one of the best ways to bring the beauty and serenity of nature indoors. Restful, cool, and fresh are words that come to mind. Because this color creates the illusion of space and distance, rooms painted blue actually look and feel larger than they are. One of the most popular colors for interior design, blue generally has a refreshing sense of tranquility. Its many shades range from cool aquamarine to soft baby blue to pale bluebell. All create wonderful effects in bedrooms and bathrooms. Blue and yellow has always been a favorite combination, but why not try a new pairing with off-white, taupe, gray, or hot pink?

Brown in its various shades is reminiscent of rich soil. It has the feeling of stability and security. It can range from gentle beige to rich, dark chocolate. A mellow and cozy color, down-to-earth brown can recall the hues of autumn or antique wood. Paler tones provide an unobtrusive backdrop to any palette, while rich tones make a bolder statement of balance and strength. Soft tones of peach or apricot combined with dark wood are stunning partners.

Yellow suggests warmth and sunshine. Different tones can remind us of springtime daffodils or sunflowers in late summer. It's an optimistic color that warms up cold rooms and offsets the gloom of

ABOVE Touches of blue in this otherwise neutral living room harmonize with the spectacular ocean view.

BELOW A hint of blue-green in this bowl partners beautifully with silver, crystal, crisp white, and rich cream.

ABOVE Brown, in its many variations, adds polish to both contemporary and traditional decorating schemes.

a windowless corner. The gentler yellow shades of sand, maize, or straw work well as a backdrop because of their easy-on-the-eyes, subtle hues. Accents of off-white, cream, cinnamon, or ginger are effective combinations. Be watchful of using a too-bright yellow, though: it can have an overwhelming energy that may be difficult on the eyes and the nerves. When used correctly, yellow is brilliant and lively, the perfect color for a room that is small, windowless, or simply in need of an uplifting color scheme. When muted, yellow has a calm, refreshing feel and can be used in virtually any room in your home.

Nature's Neutrals

White is the purest of colors. Bright white gives the feeling of cleanliness and purity. Look to nature to see how many different tones and shades of white exist: the bluish white of fresh fallen snow, the pinkish white of seashells, or the parchment-like skin of a garlic bulb. White is the color most susceptible to changes of light and shade. It's also the color that takes on the tones of surrounding hues. Pastels paired with a soft white can be a soothing combination, whereas richer colors, such as eggplant or persimmon, look crisp and

clear alongside clean white. Most shades of white—from the earthier ivory to the brightest blue-white—complement a natural palette with a sense of clarity and freshness. When you're choosing a shade of white, examine the fabric swatch or paint chip in all kinds of light and compare it with other whites to make sure you have the right shade.

Gray is a cool color that's often thought of as somber. Gray can be found in nature in an icy mountaintop, pebbles on a beach, a slab of slate, a mound of charcoal, or the color of the sky on a wintry day. The shades can range from silvery gray to pewter to a warmer taupe tinged with brown. Gray adds cool sophistication but is also a perfect backdrop for other natural shades. Mix gray with pale pastels, such as pink and yellow: it will tone them down and give your room a modern look.

ABOVE Rich mahogany and several shades of white combine in this African-inspired master bedroom.

Vibrants: Nature's Accent Colors

Red stimulates a strong emotional and physical response. A powerful color, it can be exciting and take center stage in any room. Medical tests have proven that red can increase the heart rate and raise body temperature. Nature uses red profusely—the vibrant red of

ABOVE Orange can be a bold, stimulating color best used for accents. Toned down as in this sofa, it becomes a rich, neutral shade that warms this outdoor room.

RIGHT Red and green are complementary colors on the color wheel and work well together, especially in these toned-down shades of orange-red and sage green.

strawberries, the earthy red of clay, the burgundy of grapes. Just as in nature, red works as an accent for a variety of neutrals. Team it with sandy beige, pale blue, muted greens, or soft yellows. It creates a warm, welcoming atmosphere in a dining room or a boost of artificial "heat" in a north-facing bedroom or study. As with other strong colors, a little red makes a big impact—painting one wall or adding a couple of red accessories can alter the look of a room.

Orange is the color of enthusiasm. Orange can range from bright yellow-orange to deep terra-cotta and rust to soft corals. As a dominant color in your design, it can evoke earthy terra-cotta pots or the autumn bounty of gourds and pumpkins. Pale orange can be cheerful and whimsical, while a bright tangerine can be comforting.

Living with Neutrals

A neutral color scheme can be both dramatic and sophisticated. Because its color palette is limited, a monochromatic décor is easy to pull together and extremely effective. It evokes an aura of calm tranquility or urban sophistication. It reflects light and makes the

ABOVE This neutral color scheme subtly combines tones of gray, white, and taupe with dark brown wood accents.

room visually expand. Neutrals and naturals rely on texture, pattern, and contrast for depth and interest. Suede, wool, or cashmere weaves or rich woods are wonderful counterbalances. With neutrals serving as a backdrop for the colors around them, it's easy to change the look of a room by varying accessories, such as curtains or cushions. For the best results, use one dominant neutral for the furniture, window treatments, or walls. Pull in a darker neutral for contrast, then add a third or even a fourth neutral to round out the look. If the room seems bland, give it some pattern or a shot of color with fabric, rugs, or wall coverings. Natural materials work well with these neutral tones. Use a pale wood floor with other tones of wood, cork, slate, stone, sisal, linen, bamboo, and wicker.

New Ways with Naturals

Natural color schemes are easy to refresh by using them in new, unexpected combinations. Try an updated pairing of burnt ochre with twilight blue, pewter with purple, chocolate brown with red, or cream with plum.

ABOVE The brown, gold, and orange stripes in this hallway runner make effective partners for the wood floors and furniture.

OPPOSITE A stone and iron dining table and chairs are highlighted by the intense gold tones of the seat cushions and walls.

The Cultural Effects of Color

Culture and history both have an effect on how we react to color. For instance, in America and much of Europe, blue is a perennial favorite, while red ranks first in some other countries, such as Spain and Japan. Western brides dress in joyful white, which is a mourning color in some Far Eastern societies.

Color trends also vary from era to era and generation to generation. You might wince at the pink and black of a 1950s bathroom or the avocado green and harvest gold of a 1970s kitchen. Yet what seems outmoded to some of us appears fresh and new to younger generations. Thanks to the Internet, color trends and international inspiration are only a click away. Let these design influences inspire you to incorporate new color combinations into your décor.

Defining Space with Color

You can use color to manipulate the way a room is perceived visually as well as emotionally. Because warm colors appear to advance, walls painted in warm tones seem closer together and make a room feel more intimate. Remember, the larger the area, the more intense a strong color will appear. Conversely, cool tones and neutrals appear to recede and can be used to open up a smaller space. If a ceiling feels low, paint it a cool tint of white to make it look taller; if it's too high, use a warmer shade. These tricks can be used in other ways. For example, if you'd love to use bright yellow in a small living room, but worry about its effect, you can use a paler shade of the same color, or paint only one wall of the room in the bold shade. In fact, painting walls a contrasting color or shade can highlight special features of a room. A muted color on the walls around a painting will direct the eye toward the stronger colors of the artwork.

Light and Color

The lighting in a room is one of the most important influences on your choice of color scheme. Light can change the way the color appears to the eye. How often have you fallen in love with a paint chip or a fabric swatch, only to bring it home and see it in a completely different way? If you stand next to a window, you may see the color in its true hue. Even that will be affected by the weather outside and the time of day. For instance, natural light will appear different on a foggy, rainy day,

LIVE WISE, LIVE WELL

Dryers account for a large amount of home energy use and carbon emissions. To be more environmentally friendly, try using a clothesline instead. A household washing 200 loads per year and letting nature dry them could prevent one ton of CO_2 emissions. What could be better than using the most natural dryer of all, the sun? Your linens will last longer, and they'll smell fresher, too. You'll also love those lower utility bills. Even if you line-dry laundry just once a week, or during the summer, you'll still be making a significant difference.

LEFT The light-color furniture and flooring intensify the level of natural light this room receives from the windows.

a clear winter afternoon, at noon on a sunny summer day, or in the fading light at sunset. Make sure you consider this when choosing a color. Paint some test samples on big sheets of cardboard; drape a piece of fabric over a curtain rod or the arm of the sofa. Watch how the colors change depending on the position of the sun. Should you adjust the shade or tone because of the light? Rooms with northern exposure will be filled with bluer, cooler light, which weakens warm colors

ABOVE The rug, pillows, and upholstery in this sitting room offer different types of tactile and visual experiences that enrich the design.

but intensifies cool hues. Rooms facing south will have a warmer, yellowish light. In addition, pale or neutral furniture and walls will make a room with poor light appear brighter. The same white hue can seem more intense in a room with large windows or grayish in a room with little light. Colors interact in complex ways, and their selection is very personal. It's important to experiment with potential colors and not make a final decision until you've observed them in the room in which they will be used.

Texture

A creative mix of materials brings a natural decorating scheme to life. Look at all the different textures in nature: the roughness of tree bark, the smooth skin of a leaf, the rough edge of a stone. All of these combine to make nature infinitely interesting, transforming itself every season and hour of the day. With the pared-down and simplified color schemes of a natural home, fabric, material, and weave make a significant impact. A mix of textures plays upon the senses and adds another layer of complexity and sophistication. As with every aspect of decorating, mixing veneers, weights, and surfaces involves a balancing act. To give a room a distinctive character, you might let one texture predominate the room, but the right contrast of different textures can make the scheme more intriguing. Texture can be added with fabric, too: a silky Egyptian cotton, rough muslin, soft and fuzzy cashmere, or finely woven linen—all produce a visual as well as a tactile sensation. Tactile interest can come from any material or surface that is coarse or smooth, hard or soft, matte or shiny. Coarse or matte surfaces, such as stone, rough-hewn wood, wicker, corduroy, wool, or terra-cotta absorb light and sound. Glossy and smooth surfaces, including metal, silk, and glass, all reflect light.

Texture also affects color. A coarsely textured surface tones down the intensity of a paint color and imparts subtle variations. By contrast, high-gloss surfaces increase the intensity of a color. Think how the gray color of a tweed jacket looks weathered and muted. On a silk shirt, the same gray color would look shimmery and more intense—a completely different appearance. Every room has existing textural elements—a stone fireplace, brass hardware—that you'll want to consider when planning your design.

BELOW The mix of textures visible in nature should inspire you to create the same effect in your own home.

Spatial Tricks

To start adding texture, assess your room's needs. Does it lack warmth? Does it feel too closed? Texture affects a room spatially: coarse or matte surfaces will make a room feel cozier and smaller. A living room of only glossy surfaces can seem cold and impersonal, but add a knitted cashmere throw or roughly textured muslin pillows and it will seem warm and inviting. Smooth surfaces do the reverse—they make a room look larger and brighter. A family room that feels too small, for instance, may benefit from the addition of a mirror or glass-top table. Light reflected off either object will brighten the space.

Monochromatic or featureless rooms can be vastly improved by adding textures. Eco-friendly wallpaper comes in a variety of textures, from faux grass or soft fleece to real fabrics, such as muslin or canvas. Look for a Greenguard or Oeko-Tek certification

THINK GREEN

Green Carpet Tips

Why not give old carpets a second life? Cut them into small pieces and turn them into area rugs. Donate them to an animal shelter to line cages. Wrap them around pieces of wood and create scratching posts for kittens. Use them in the garden as mulch or between rows of plants to prevent weeds. Find a carpet reclamation partner in your area through Carpet America Recovery Effort (CARE). Since 2002, CARE has diverted more than 3.6 billion pounds of carpet from landfills. (For more information on carpet recycling, visit *www.carpetrecovery.org*.)

RIGHT The high gloss of the silver paint on the table not only intensifies the color, but also reflects light to make subtle variations in tone, depending on the time of day.

for low-VOC wallpaper and textiles (*www.greenguard.org* and *www.oeko-tex.com*). Paint can be rag rolled or sponged; plaster can be tinted to give it more interesting surface variations. Architectural details, such as cornices, tiles, or moldings, provide a room with added tactile richness.

Window treatments are another opportunity to add texture. Natural materials, such as bamboo or woven woods, serve as a foil for monochromatic color schemes. Texture can be enhanced by the way

fabric is hung. Pleating on a pillow or draperies, for example, creates a play of light and shadow. Combine layers of rough- and smooth-weave fabrics or mix fabrics and shades to show off different textures.

On the floor, carpets can be smooth or nubby weaves. Natural fibers—rush, coir, sisal, or cork—add warmth and an intricate texture that can ground the room. Quarry tiles, ceramic tiles, marble, and slate make a room cooler. Varying the materials can make the effect more interesting.

CHAPTER 4

On the Surface

Textures and finishes in your home

Walk barefoot across a ceramic-tile floor, run your hand over a burnished wood table, chop a pile of vegetables on a bamboo countertop: the pleasure involved in each of these activities has a lot to do with the surfaces you've chosen. Textures, weaves, veneers, finishes—each plays an important role in your home.

BEFORE YOU CHOOSE THE MATERIALS for your floors, walls, windows, and furniture, ask yourself some questions. First, what is the function of the room, and how will your choice of surfaces affect it? Is it a place that gets lots of traffic, such as a family room or kitchen? Obviously, the surfaces you choose for a busy area of your home should be durable and easy to clean. Another significant consideration is comfort. A hard surface—such as a tile or laminate floor—can certainly be sturdy and a breeze to clean, but may not be comfortable for young children or an avid cook who spends long hours standing in the kitchen.

Next is the question of cost: in some cases, professional installation can add a hefty price tag to certain materials. Are you a do-it-yourself kind of person? Some products, such as vinyl floor tile, can be installed with a bit of basic training. Many home improvement stores offer free classes in how to install the products they sell. This can be a great option if you are on a budget. Other products, such as costly granite countertops, are best left to the professionals.

OPPOSITE The appeal of wood furniture and floors is universal and fits into any decorating scheme, whether it's contemporary or rustic.

THINK GREEN

Clean Sweep

Whenever possible, use a broom or carpet sweeper instead of an energy-hogging vacuum. Brooms allow quick and easy cleanup, and they don't disturb the peace. Carpet sweepers don't require a dustpan and work well on low-pile carpeting as well as hard floors. Prevention is the best green care for all types of flooring. The cleaner you keep them, the less harsh chemicals you'll need.

TOP RIGHT A casual arrangement of white mums pairs well with a natural design scheme.

BOTTOM RIGHT Inspiration for surface choices can be found in the beauty and texture of the natural world.

What type of maintenance will the surface require? Is it easily stained? Does it have to be sealed periodically? Check to see if the adhesives, stains, and other chemicals necessary release volatile organic compounds (VOCs), which are harmful to humans and the environment. Today, there are a number of low- or no-VOC alternatives, labeled as such on retail shelves. However, there is no standardization for consistent labeling. Ask your retailer, contractor, or installer for more information on the safety of the products you choose.

Flooring

Selecting a flooring material is one of the most important decisions you will make when decorating a room. There are materials that can enhance a natural decorating scheme and the overall look of the room. Flooring also provides a unique tactile component to the design. There are several natural and eco-friendly choices available in a wide range of finishes and materials. Consider the principles of color and texture

ABOVE Wood flooring can be bleached and stained to a light color that is the perfect background for this red-and-cream design scheme.

and relate them to your selection and the rest of the room. Select the highest quality that you can afford, and avoid bargain materials that you will need to replace in several years.

Bamboo

Bamboo is actually a rapidly growing grass. Because it replenishes itself so quickly, bamboo is a very eco-friendly material. The woody stems are cut and sliced into long strips, which are laminated together into veneers. Bamboo is available in two basic grain patterns: horizontal, which shows the nodes of the grass, and vertical, made by gluing together narrow strips. Vertical-grain bamboo is more stable, which makes it a better choice for damp locations, such as kitchens and bathrooms. Sold in strips or planks up to 6 inches (15 centimeters) wide, it is available either finished or unfinished. Bamboo is also available in tongue-and-groove planks that snap together. Look for the VOC rating if it is prefinished. If you plan on having the material finished in your home, use a low-VOC sealant. Under ideal conditions, a quality bamboo floor can last as long as 50 years.

Wood

Wood flooring enhances the décor of any room, providing a timeless beauty and built-in value to your home. Wood floors have come a long way in the past few years, with more styles, colors, and species of wood available than ever before. Whether you're looking for traditional oak, rustic pine, or repurposed barn wood, there are a wealth of finishes to fit your room and needs. When properly finished, wood is one of the easiest floor surfaces to keep clean. Vacuuming is the best way to remove surface dust and dirt before it gets worked into the finish and dulls its luster.

LIVE WISE, LIVE WELL

Greener Floor Care

Avoid wet-mopping hardwood, laminate, bamboo, and linoleum, because large amounts of water can damage them. Damp-mop them instead using a microfiber mop or sponge mop. Use a 50/50 mix of white vinegar and water for light cleaning or a plant-oil-based floor cleaner for heavier grime.

LEFT The rich patina of age can be seen in this recycled wood floor.

If you live in an older home, it's possible that you may have wood flooring hiding under existing carpeting. Although it may need sanding and resurfacing, the results can be well worth the work. Another option for an antique look is to purchase reclaimed or recycled wood from old structures that has been refashioned into flooring.

Because it is a natural resource, wood is both potentially renewable and recyclable. When purchasing new hardwood flooring, check for Forest Stewardship Council (FSC)-certified wood. Locally produced wood cuts down on pollution from transportation. When installing flooring, make sure that you use low- or no-VOC adhesives, paint, or finishes.

ABOVE This unusual wood surface is inlaid with two different tones for a striped effect.

Engineered Wood

Engineered floors, also known as wood-veneer flooring, consist of a thin layer of hardwood glued to layers of less-expensive plywood or pine in a process that actually makes them more stable than solid wood. Because just a thin layer of decorative hardwood is peeled from the trunk of a tree, these products help delay the harvesting of mature trees. Some engineered wood comes in planks that can be glued or nailed to the subfloor. Other types are not attached to the subfloor; they are referred to as "floating," a quality that allows them to be used over a wide variety of surfaces. Installation is quick and relatively easy, and you can receive directions on how to do the job at your local home improvement store. Check that the product has a low-VOC rating. The best choices for engineered wood are those that are FSC-certified and manufactured with no or low levels of formaldehyde-based glues. Engineered wood can be refinished, although not as many times as real wood.

Laminate Floors

Laminate floors can mimic the look of stone, tile, or wood, but they are actually a photographic image impregnated with melamine and bonded under high pressure to a hard, transparent layer. They are very durable and easy to maintain, which accounts for their wide popularity. Laminate floors are usually "floating" (not attached

LEFT Engineered-wood floors are chosen by many homeowners because they are long lasting and easy to install.

to a subfloor) and often have fiberboard cores made with urea-formaldehyde binders. Because a damaged laminate floor cannot be repaired like wood or engineered wood, be certain you have a good warranty. Some laminate floors feature FSC-certified wood cores and low urea-formaldehyde emissions.

Cork

First used in the late 1800s, cork has proven to be a reliable and durable surface. Made from the peeled or stripped bark of cork oak trees, it is one of the more sustainable surfaces available today. Cork acts as a sound and cold insulator, is resistant to fire and moisture, and provides a resilient surface for flooring. Some cork products are solid, while others are glued to a wood substrate. Cork is available in tiles, planks, and sheeting in a variety of shades to fit most decorating schemes. Make sure to use organic or low-VOC adhesives. This may be a do-it-yourself project for many homeowners, so check with your local home improvement store for how-to workshops.

BELOW If you plan to use furniture on casters, the durability and hardness of your flooring will be important. Vinyl and cork may show dents and impressions, but concrete, wood, and bamboo will not.

Ceramic Tile

Tile remains the most popular surface for both kitchens and bathrooms. It is both rugged and long lasting. Ceramic tile starts with clay and is formed into a material called bisque. The bisque is shaped into tiles and is fired in a kiln at extremely high temperatures. Because ceramic tile is naturally porous, it is usually glazed to seal and harden the surface. Grout should also be sealed with a low-toxic sealant.

Apart from its relatively low cost, the main value of ceramic tile is that it can be formed into an infinite variety of colors and shapes. Used for floors, backsplashes, and countertops, it is possible to pick up a theme and carry it to several surfaces in the same space. Also on the plus side, tile is long lasting and easy to maintain. The downsides are that tile is cold underfoot, noisy, and a fragile object dropped on it can break.

Concrete

Concrete can make a surprisingly beautiful surface in your home. It can be left in its natural state or dyed to complement the décor in your space. Before installing a concrete floor, be certain that the underlying structures in your home can support its weight. If you are building a new home, you can use polished concrete for floors on grade level. Concrete can be cold, and care must be taken not to drop heavy objects on it as this can cause cracking or denting. If you stand for long periods of time in front of a sink, you may want to cover the area with a slip-resistant rug. As with any hard surface, there is a risk that

ABOVE The light-color flooring makes this room look wonderfully expansive and airy, but may require extra care to keep it free of dirt, stains, and scuff marks.

children or the elderly may be hurt if they fall. Installation is best left to a professional. Concrete does crack, so if you are a perfectionist, it may not be the best choice for you.

Slate

Slate is a fine-grained stone available in a range of shades from grays to browns to purples. It is highly resistant to damage providing that it is installed on top of a solid subfloor. With its distinctive surface, ease of installation, and natural slip resistance, it can be a fine choice for a kitchen or bathroom. Slate may need to be sealed depending on the source and porousness of the particular slate.

Linoleum

Linoleum is considered an eco-friendly product because it's made from natural and renewable ingredients, including linseed oil and wood "flour," pine resins, and limestone dust. Unlike

LEFT Linoleum flooring, a man-made product made from linseed oil, wood, pine, limestone, and other ingredients, is available in tiles and allows for colorful floor patterns. It is also available in interlocking panels.

petroleum-based vinyl flooring, linoleum does not outgas toxins such as lead, cadmium, and phthalate plasticizers. While resistant to moisture, linoleum will rot if laid on a damp floor. It is naturally antibiotic and can last as long as 40 years. Linoleum comes in dozens of colors and patterns and is sold in sheets or tiles. Some companies offer interlocking panels that can be installed by a do-it-yourselfer.

ABOVE Combining different countertop surfaces is a popular decorating choice. This island provides a warm contrast to the white marble surfaces around the perimeter of the room.

Countertops

Many of the same materials used for flooring may also be used for countertops. The decorative and long-lasting qualities of ceramic tile make it a good option for backsplashes and countertops. It's especially important that grout is sealed in this application to protect against stains and spills. You might want to choose a darker grout to avoid constant cleaning. Wood also makes a striking countertop application. Consider reclaimed or recycled lumber from sustainably harvested varieties. Just like wood flooring, wood countertops need to be sealed. You can also choose solid-surface countertops, which consist of a single, seamless piece of material. Solid-surface materials include quartz products, plastic laminates, and an exciting new range of recycled options.

Wood and Bamboo

Despite its vulnerability to moisture, scratches, and stains, butcher block remains a time-honored countertop material. Usually made of hard or rock maple, butcher block can warp if exposed to water.

It should be washed gently and periodically treated with natural mineral oil. If you're buying wood countertops, look for FSC-certified or salvaged wood. Wood counters will eventually show some scratches and stains, but most imperfections can be sanded or left alone to enhance the natural character of the wood. Bamboo is another good choice for its durability and sustainability. Popular in recent years for flooring, bamboo kitchen utensils, cutting boards, and countertops are becoming increasingly popular. Like wood, it needs sealing to protect it from water.

ABOVE Wood and bamboo make attractive countertops, but are vulnerable to water exposure, scratches, and stains. Sanding and sealing help to maintain their surfaces.

Natural surfaces enhance the look of a room

Concrete

Concrete is an intriguing and versatile material that can be formed into any number of interesting shapes. Just right for ultra-contemporary kitchens, it also provides a mellow, weathered look that works with country or European-farmhouse styles. Concrete is often used in its natural state, a gray hue that mellows over time.

Tints are available in a number of colors, from earthy tones, such as ivory, clay, or beige, to vivid and deeply saturated shades. Finishes can go from rough to glossy. It can be inlaid with small stones, bits of shiny metal, or colored glass. Concrete counters are resistant to heat and scratching, but do require periodic sealing. Fabrication and installation should be done by an expert.

Stone

Slate, soapstone, and granite are among the most expensive materials you can use for surfaces in your home, but their beauty and luminosity make them worth the investment. Picking a stone surface from a location close to your home helps to keep the material more eco-friendly. These materials are heavy, and you need to be sure the floor or cabinets that support them are able to bear the weight. While slate can be used for countertops, it is softer than other stones, and you should avoid sharp corners, because they could chip. Stone countertops should be professionally installed.

Counters can be the focal point in the kitchen or bathroom

Granite is a dense, variegated rock available in a variety of colors and is one of the most highly coveted countertop surfaces. Elegant and beautiful, granite is heavy, and a considerable amount of energy is required to quarry, transport, and prepare the surface prior to installation. Using a stone quarried close to home helps to minimize some of the environmental impact. Used stone is available and may be found at garage sales, auctions, or local salvage yards. Check to see if the stone requires sealing; if so, pick one with no or low VOCs. Using a mechanical rather than adhesive method of installation will allow easier removal and increase the potential for reuse of the slab.

Soapstone is actually steatite stone, but was given its common name because of its texture, which resembles soap. Naturally gray, soapstone is a relatively soft stone but is water resistant. Stains or discoloration remain on the surface, and can be sanded or washed to remove. Maintenance includes regular treatment with mineral oil. Scratches can be sanded smooth.

Slate is less porous than marble, durable, and may require sealing, depending on the source and porousness of the particular slate. It's available in black, gray, and shades of green and red. Because it is stone, it looks luxurious, but it can scratch and chip easily.

OPPOSITE Engineered stone is popular in bathrooms because it has the look of real stone but is lower in cost and relatively maintenance free.

Marble can be expensive, and therefore might not be the most economical selection for use on every surface in a kitchen. A more reasonable alternative might be an inset for your pastry station rather than the entire countertop. Marble stains easily, requires a lot of maintenance, and must be resealed regularly. Installation requires professional tools and skills.

Engineered stone is composed primarily of crushed quartz mixed with resin and pigments, and presents a durable yet beautiful surface. It is available in a variety of colors, textures, and edge options. Some styles even have the appearance of marble or stone. It does not require sealing, and is resistant to heat, staining, and scratches. Although its cost is similar to natural stone, it may be worth the money if you want a low-maintenance, more uniform look than natural stone can provide.

Metals

Stainless steel has long been used in restaurant kitchens and has recently come of age as a surface used in homes. It pairs beautifully with other materials, especially wood and marble. It's a good surface to use in damp areas and can be formed into an integral sink and countertop configuration. Stainless steel is durable and easy to clean. Depending on its thickness and formulation, it can be vulnerable to stains and corrosion; look for high-gauge stainless steel with a high chromium and nickel content.

Copper is prone to dents and tends to react to acids by tarnishing. Sealed copper squares are more durable than sheet copper. It must be installed over a solid surface, such as plywood or your existing counter. Seams can be soldered to avoid cracks. It is relatively easy to install.

LEFT The huge trend in stainless steel appliances has led to a demand for matching countertops. They are heat- and moisture-resistant and look great in both modern and traditional kitchen designs.

Eco-Friendly Options

Recycled aluminum is used in tiles and countertops; custom-applied patinas or colored powdercoats are available. The tiles can also be used on floors and walls. The EPA states that the total amount of aluminum in the municipal solid waste (MSW) stream was 3.6 million tons in 2015. The largest source is aluminum used in beverage and other containers. When aluminum is recycled, toxic metals and dirt are removed.

Recycled glass surfaces are available made with recycled glass, sometimes mixed with concrete, or combined with porcelain in an epoxy resin binder. The glass may come from lightbulbs, windshields, and bottles. Glass is nonporous, hard, and heat resistant, but it can crack if something heavy is dropped on it. It is sanitary and easy to clean. It is possible to install lighting under some glass countertops for a dramatic focal point in your kitchen. This material is best used in a backsplash application to avoid fingerprints and possible breakage.

Recycled paper counters can be made from recycled paper impregnated with recycled plastic resin. It's heat and stain resistant and has a similar look and feel to soapstone. Thicknesses range from 1 to 2 inches (2.5 to 5 centimeters). Like wood, it can be scratched and should be protected with a cutting board.

BELOW LEFT Recycled glass comes from many sources, including lightbulbs and auto windshields.

BELOW RIGHT Countertops made out of composites of recycled paper and other materials make a good eco-friendly choice for kitchens.

Terrazzo is a smooth, multicolor surface traditionally made of small chips of marble mixed into cement. Today an epoxy binder is often used as a base for marble and recycled materials such as glass and metal shapes or medallions. Counters can be colored or stained to match cabinets or painted wall surfaces. No sealing is required.

Wall Treatments

Walls are the most noticeable surfaces in your home and can contribute to the natural feeling you seek to emphasize. Anything from a simple paint finish to wallpaper to special effects, such as

THINK GREEN

Clean Green

Replace sponges, disposable dusting cloths, and paper towels with microfiber cloths. Microfiber's scrubbing power means you can avoid using harsh cleaning solutions, and fewer chemicals means less pollution. Because microfiber cloths can be washed hundreds of times, you save resources by purchasing fewer disposable products.

LEFT Many flaws in a wall surface can be hidden by using fabric wall treatments. Check out natural fabrics such as cotton, linen, and grasscloth applied with nontoxic adhesives.

murals, can make a dramatic statement. Neutral paint and wallpaper provide a backdrop for furniture and artwork. Before deciding on a color or fabric, note the condition of your walls, the effect they have on the room, and their current surface treatments. You can fill small holes and cracks yourself using joint compound purchased at a home improvement store. Larger defects may need to be fixed by a professional. If you currently have wallpaper, it should be removed before painting or applying new wallpaper. Paneling can be removed, but expect to repair holes and whatever other surprises you may find once the paneling is lifted. Painting over paneling can be an economical and eco-friendly alternative; make sure you prepare the surface by lightly sanding, and—in most cases—applying a low-VOC primer prior to painting the surface.

Next, measure the effect you are seeking with the amount of work you are willing to do to get there. Brighter colors may be fun for now,

ABOVE The paint and wall covering in this open kitchen and living room provide the perfect neutral backdrop for woods, leather, and fabrics.

OPPOSITE Wallpaper incorporates color, texture, and pattern into your home. Look for recycled or natural paper with eco-friendly backings.

Wall coverings incorporate color, pattern, and texture into your home

but are you willing to apply the many coats of paint it may take to cover them in the future? If you paint walls white, are you willing to keep up with cleaning the many spots that come from children and pets?

There are many faux finishes and painted effects that you can learn from classes at your local home improvement store. If you are seeking a natural feel, consider colors such as greens, browns, and blues. Pick up some paint chips, bring them home, and try the color before you buy. If you still aren't sure, buy a quart can of paint and try a patch on the wall. Generally, flat paint is best used for the ceiling and walls; easy-to-clean semi-gloss is recommended for wood trim; and in areas prone to scuff marks and other soiling, you may want to consider a satin finish.

RIGHT The rough texture of the distressed wood table partners well with the natural stone color of the wall and the pumpkin corduroy chair.

Eco-Smart Paints

The type of paint you choose has a significant effect on the environment in your home. Most interior paints are either alkyd-resin (oil-based) or latex (water-based) products. Alkyd paints require solvents to thin and clean paintbrushes, and they are both toxic and combustible. Alkyd paints also outgas VOCs that are toxic and can also be carcinogenic. VOCs can be released for years after the paint is applied. Latex paints have a short drying time, are generally nontoxic, and brushes and equipment can be cleaned with soap and water.

When purchasing paints, look for low or no-VOC products. Check for any other chemical content as well—avoid paints with formaldehyde or with notices that they are neurotoxic. Ask for information about the product's safety. Paint applied before 1978 may contain lead; before you sand or otherwise disturb it, double-check with the EPA at *www.epa.gov/lead*.

ABOVE Most paint companies have lines of eco-friendly paints in an ever-expanding variety of colors and finishes.

Alternative Paints

Alternative eco-friendly organic paints also include natural milk paints and products made from organic pigments. One option is a nontoxic paint with milk protein, lime, clay, and earth pigments. There are also soy-based paints and those made with clay and minerals.

RIGHT Prints or photographs of natural materials such as flowers, leaves, or stones are striking additions to wall surfaces.

Some consider the organic paints healthier because they allow the walls to breathe and are biodegradable. Natural pigments have a slightly uneven coverage on the walls, so if you are a perfectionist, practice using them on a test board first.

Other Surface Coverings

Clay plaster is made from natural ingredients, such as water, colored sand, and ground marble, and has a breathable, textured surface in warm, natural colors. It's easy to apply yourself to previously painted walls with a sanded primer that lets the clay bond to the surface.

Wall coverings are now available made from environmentally friendly fibers, such as recycled paper and water-based or vegetable-dye inks. They contain no vinyl, PVC, or VOCs. Some have biodegradable backings and others are pre-pasted. Grass cloth, hemp, woven raffia, burlap, and other weaves are available as natural coverings. Use solvent-free adhesives to minimize releasing toxic compounds into your home.

ABOVE Natural paints are made from vegetable and mineral ingredients that are safe for the environment. The harmful release of toxic fumes is kept to a minimum.

CHAPTER 5

Kitchens
and Bathrooms

Natural designs for hardworking spaces

The kitchen and bathroom are the busiest areas of the house. They are also the rooms most likely to benefit from a redesign that is both eco-friendly and efficient. From energy-saving appliances to green cabinets to flow-control faucets, today's kitchens and bathrooms are inspired by nature and dedicated to its well-being—as well as yours.

THERE IS GOOD NEWS APLENTY ABOUT going green in the kitchen and bathroom. Not too long ago, eco-conscious home products had a reputation for being expensive and difficult to find. Thanks to a recent surge of interest in eco-friendly living, manufacturers have responded by introducing a wide range of items in nearly every category and price point that are both energy-efficient and stylish. From Energy Star–rated appliances that require 10 to 50 percent less water and energy, to light-emitting diode (LED) fixtures, to toxin-free paints, adhesives, countertops, cabinetry, and flooring, your kitchen and bathroom can be high on style and function and low on environmental impact.

As in any remodeling project, you'll want to do your research. Familiarize yourself with the latest innovations in the marketplace before determining just how green you want—or are able—to go. To help you decide, it makes sense to consult with a design professional who is knowledgeable about eco-friendly design. He or she can help you make your dream a reality.

OPPOSITE A sleek, professional-style range tops many kitchen remodel wish lists. Today, you can customize the equipment to suit your cooking style—and even combine gas and electric fuel in the same model.

Working with a Designer

If you choose to work with a design professional, expect to be interviewed at the beginning of the planning stage. He or she will want to get to know you and whoever else will be using the new bathroom or kitchen. Your designer isn't being nosy. He or she simply wants to understand your lifestyle, habits, basic requirements, and dreams for your new room. The designer will also make a sketch of the existing space to get an idea of what works and what doesn't. This rough drawing may include any adjacent areas that might be considered for expansion, such as a pantry, hallway, closet, or small room. If you'd like to explore eco-friendly options, it pays to find a contractor, architect, or interior designer who is knowledgeable and committed to green design. Listen to their suggestions and work together to map out a realistic and affordable plan that satisfies all your needs. That way, you won't have to retrofit low-toxin or energy-saving products in the future.

BELOW A sprightly combination of navy blue and white is carried throughout this kitchen, highlighted by a generous center island with a white marble top and navy bead-board paneling.

If you plan on being your own designer, don't assume that just because you live there you'll instinctively know what has to be done to transform an old room into a fabulous new space. Analyze your

LEFT In the same kitchen, a built-in banquette reverses the color combination and provides a cozy place for family dining.

THINK GREEN

Finding Green Professionals

Look at websites and magazine articles for names of green builders or designers. Check the Green Building Certification Institute's website, *www.gbci.org*, and click on the LEED AP directory to find professionals near you that have been LEED certified. That means they have been accredited by the institute as having a thorough understanding of green building practices. Other websites such as *www.lowimpactliving.com* also have listings of architects and builders who specialize in green projects.

RIGHT The plants, flowers, and ornate shell mirror in this bathroom add a touch of nature that softens the hard edges of the cabinets and counters.

 LIVE WISE, LIVE WELL

ABOVE Sea sponges add a touch of the natural world to this eco-friendly bathroom.

Inspired by Nature

Simple ways to bring nature into your decorating scheme:

- Turn a windowsill into an herb garden by adding terra-cotta pots filled with basil, rosemary, thyme, and sage.
- Show off individual blooms from your garden by displaying them in wine glasses.
- Decorate a pot rack with garlands of braided garlic.
- Make a mini conservatory in your kitchen with hanging pots of ivy and masses of flowering plants.
- Use dish soap or hand cream with fragrances, such as lemon verbena, rosemary, mint, and lavender.
- Set the table with natural plates and cutlery made out of bamboo.
- Use wicker baskets and covered boxes to store potatoes, onions, and loose gadgets in the kitchen and laundry or towels in the bathroom.
- Display lemons, apples, or pomegranates in beautiful bowls on the kitchen table and island.
- Hang framed prints of flowers on bathroom or kitchen walls.
- Use shells to hold soap or sponges next to the sink.
- Make potpourri with flowers and herbs from your garden, and store it in a pretty box on a bathroom shelf.
- Choose chairs or benches made out of natural materials, such as rattan, wicker, or bamboo.
- Paint the walls one of the colors from nature that inspire you.

lifestyle. Talk to everyone in the household. Ask each family member what they dislike about the present space, what their dream design might be, and what aspects of the space they'd prefer to remain the same. Approach the project in the same analytical manner as a professional who understands design and can be objective about what is required.

Natural Kitchens

Making the most efficient use of the space you have available is the first and most important step in an eco-friendly kitchen. For example, it may be tempting to make your kitchen bigger and to add bells and whistles, such as a second dishwasher or a larger refrigerator. It's important to weigh your need for such features against their significant space requirements and energy costs.

BELOW An enormous dual-surface island makes food prep, cooking, and informal dining a breeze.

How to Start

1. Create a design notebook. It's useful to keep all your ideas and records in one place. Buy a loose-leaf binder and use it to organize

LEFT If you have the room, including a walk-in pantry is a convenient way to get cans and boxes off the shelves and organized in an out-of-the-way area.

everything from magazine clippings to photos of the old kitchen (important when you choose to resell the house), notes, contracts, business cards, sample plans, color charts, and fabric samples. Keep track of all the research you've done on green products; note the sources and prices. This will help you remember what you liked if you have to order things in the future. The file should be comprehensive, but not too clumsy to carry when you visit showrooms, stores, or home centers.

2. Analyze the existing kitchen. Decide what you really want to gain by remodeling. You might begin by asking the most obvious question: "What's wrong with the existing kitchen?" Maybe you and your partner enjoy cooking together, but the floor plan was designed to work for only one cook. Perhaps storage is inadequate or the appliances are using too much energy. Consider questions such as "Is the size of my family likely to grow or shrink in the near future?" If the kids are heading for college soon, you might not need a large-capacity refrigerator. Likewise, if this is your first house and you expect to move on as your family grows, it might be wise to hold onto working appliances and spend only a modest amount of money, time, and energy on cosmetic changes.

Other Questions to Ask Yourself

Really think about the kitchen use. How many members of the family cook frequently? Note other ways that everyone uses the kitchen. How convenient is it to prepare food, reach necessary utensils, and clean up? Are people always bumping into each other? Is the traffic pattern interrupted when cabinet or appliance doors are open? Is there enough storage? If you keep kitchen items in other areas of the house, such as the garage or basement, perhaps it's time to analyze how you can increase storage capacity in the kitchen. What is the condition of the existing materials and appliances? How old are they? Are the appliances energy efficient? Are the walls, floor, and countertops in reasonably good condition?

Make a wish list. In addition to the basic elements, make a list of all the special features you would like in your kitchen. This is a good time to write down what green issues matter most to you. If you have high utility bills, you might want to replace all your old appliances with new, energy-efficient models. If you like to cook but lack a kitchen fan, you might want to invest in a new ventilation system. Once your wish list is complete, that's the time to look for areas to trim if your budget is tight. Instead of a granite countertop, you might choose a fabricated lookalike that is both affordable and eco-friendly.

LEFT The diamond pattern on these glass-front cabinets is one of many unique details in this kitchen.

Use the dollars saved for something that can't be faked—such as energy-efficient windows.

Creating Functional Space

Your available space and budget will dictate the size of your new kitchen. However, you can establish an efficient layout no matter what the dimensions are if you employ the "work triangle"—positioning the range, refrigerator, and sink to form the three points of a triangle that are no less than 4 feet (1.2 meters) and no more than 9 feet (2.7 meters) apart. Less space between appliances makes the workspace too cramped; more space wastes steps and energy.

Traditionally, kitchen layouts have been considered to be most efficient when they are based on this work triangle. However, as kitchens have become multifunctional living spaces with separate cooktops, wall ovens, microwaves, and more, it's important to be flexible in your design. Instead, focus on the work zones or activity centers in your kitchen. Choose the shape that best suits the way you want to use your space.

OPPOSITE Frameless cabinets lend a sleek, modern feel to a kitchen.

BELOW Plate racks and open shelving for storing glassware create a fine display of collectibles in this kitchen.

Cabinets are the backbone of the kitchen; they should be strong, durable, and eco-friendly

As you consider a new layout, make sure that traffic can move easily from one spot to another in the kitchen and from the kitchen to other rooms in the house—as well as outdoors. Otherwise, carrying a hot pot from the range to the sink could put you on a collision course with children running for the back door. You can often correct a faulty traffic pattern by simply moving a door or removing a short section of wall.

Kitchen Cabinets

Choosing cabinetry is one of the biggest decisions you will make for your kitchen. In addition to the fact that their style and color set the tone for the whole room, they must also organize and store dishes, gadgets, pots, and pans. Cabinetry can involve a huge cash outlay. High-quality cabinets fitted with an assortment of organizing

 THINK GREEN

Green Cabinets

The Kitchen Cabinet Manufacturers Association has created the Environmental Stewardship Program (ESP) to help consumers identify cabinet manufacturers that have environmentally friendly products and practices. Go to *www.kcma.org/certifications/ environmental-stewardship* for a listing of cabinet companies that manufacture ESP-certified cabinets.

options can help make your kitchen more efficient—and a whole lot neater—while establishing a look for the whole room. Keep in mind that cabinetry will also consume about 40 percent of your remodeling budget, according to the National Kitchen and Bath Association. It pays to check out your options before you buy.

Cabinet Construction

There are two general types of cabinet construction: framed and frameless (also called European style).

Framed cabinets have a traditional look, with a full frame across the face of the cabinet box that may show between closed doors. This secures adjacent cabinets and strengthens wider cabinet boxes with a center rail. Hinges on framed cabinets may be visible around doors and drawers when they are closed. The door's face may be ornamented with raised or recessed panels, trimmed or framed panels, or a framed-glass panel with or without muntins, which are narrow vertical and horizontal strips of wood.

Frameless cabinets are built without a face frame for a clean, contemporary look. There's no trim or molding with this simple

OPPOSITE Framed cabinets lend a classic look to a natural home.

LEFT The mix of several different surfaces—white painted cabinets, glass fronts, and wood—adds extra flair to this kitchen.

design. Close-fitting doors cover the entire front of the box, the door faces lack ornamentation, and hinges are typically hidden inside the cabinet box.

Cabinet Materials

New kitchen cabinets can be one of the most eco-*unfriendly* elements of the house. Often, their cores, shelves, and end panels are made with plywood, particleboard, or medium density fiberboard (MDF). The adhesive that holds them together often contains urea-formaldehyde, which emits toxic vapors—also known as "outgassing." The finishes on many wood cabinets also contain urea-formaldehyde, which releases even more toxins. Some interiors are finished with melamine, a plastic resin that reduces offgassing. However, unless it covers the total cabinet surface, vapors can still be emitted.

When you're shopping for new cabinets, the best choices for interiors are those built with solid wood, followed by exterior-grade or marine-grade plywood. They're preferable to interior-grade plywood because they outgas formaldehyde at much lower levels. Other, more eco-friendly options for cabinet interiors include medium-density fiberboard, a 100-percent recycled composite-wood product, or wheatboard, which is made from compressed straw. Both use resins that do not contain formaldehyde. Look for quality construction so the cabinets will last for many years. Beware of drawers that are nailed, glued, or just stapled together. Cabinet cases should measure at least ½ inch (1.3 centimeters) thick, and all surfaces, including interiors and backs, should be finished. Adjustable shelves are another sign of quality. Make sure they measure at least ⅝ inch (1.6 centimeters) thick to prevent bowing. Look for solid hinges that don't squeak and allow doors to open fully.

If you're going to buy new standard cabinets, decrease your exposure to toxic vapors by arranging to have them delivered

BELOW These cabinets should offer enough storage to contain all cooking and serving essentials together in one area.

to your home a few weeks ahead of time. Put them in a well-ventilated garage, then open the cabinet doors and drawers to let them air out for a few weeks. You can also coat the top, bottom, and undersides of pressed-wood surfaces with a low-VOC sealant.

Reclaimed or Salvaged Wood

If you're set on wood cabinets, consider using salvaged or reclaimed wood that's taken from sources such as old barns, houses, or fallen trees. Although this is sometimes more expensive, it is a wise choice in the long run because less energy is used to produce the cabinets and you will be recycling a natural product that would otherwise have gone to waste. Reclaimed wood is usually of a finer quality than new wood because it comes from old-growth trees, which tend to warp and shrink less. The Rainforest Alliance has a certification program that certifies salvaged, reclaimed, and recycled timber that has been collected responsibly. (See the Resource Guide on page 208.) Also check local salvage, demolition, or construction companies for salvaged wood. By visiting the Internet, you can also locate stores in your area that recycle building materials.

Other Eco-Smart Materials

Bamboo, a rapidly renewable resource, is the newest and most popular green substitute for any wood product that might be in the home. Exterior parts of cabinets, such as doors and drawer fronts, are faced with bamboo, and the interiors are made of another material. Bamboo is most often available in a blond or amber color.

Interesting new cabinet materials made from recycled or renewable products are being developed all the time. For instance, some companies are using the pressed stalks of harvested Chinese sorghum for cabinet fronts. Check with your cabinet supplier to find out what's available.

BELOW Salvaged-wood surfaces can look either rustic or refined.

ABOVE White-painted cabinets with glass fronts give a crisp country look to this light-filled kitchen.

Wood Veneers

Theoretically, wood veneers are actually more eco-friendly than solid wood because they use fewer mature trees, which are in short supply. Unfortunately, many of the available veneers have been harvested in an unsustainable manner. New veneers from sustainable woods are being developed, including obeche trees from Ghana, which mimic oak, cherry, or walnut. If possible, use veneers that are FSC-certified. They may be hard to find, but more are being developed by eco-friendly cabinetmakers. If you want to buy a cabinet with wood veneer that is not FSC-certified, avoid imported exotic hardwoods and look for woods such as maple and oak.

Reuse, Renew, and Recycle

If the basic layout of your kitchen is acceptable, the most eco-conscious plan would be to reuse what you already have. Sometimes, a cosmetic makeover can make a huge difference. A thorough cleaning with an eco-friendly degreaser or wood cleaner can remove years of grease and grime on cabinets and give them a fresh look. Replacing

nonfunctioning hardware, such as hinges or drawer glides, will do a world of good. Handles and pulls may seem insignificant, but new metal or glass styles will definitely update the look. If organizing your gadgets and food has always been a problem, get some new interior, off-the-shelf or custom accessories, such as a lazy Susan in a deep corner cabinet, or pullout compartments in bottom cabinets. They'll allow you to make use of every inch of storage area.

Doors, frames, and drawer fronts on wood cabinets can be refinished or repainted using low- or no-VOC paints. There are also companies that replace or reface cabinet doors. While the price can vary depending on the number of cabinets, it will totally change the look of the kitchen without you needing to embark on a major remodeling project.

Even if you change your layout, consider whether you can retain some of the cabinets and possibly relocate them to a different spot in the kitchen—or build additional cabinets around them. As long as the styles mesh, the doors can be replaced or repainted to match. Another possibility is to save the lower cabinets and replace the uppers with open shelving. If you're removing all the cabinets, see if you can use them somewhere else in your home. A garage, family room, or home

ABOVE LEFT A kitchen's compact home office area boasts plenty of storage in these bamboo built-in units.

ABOVE RIGHT These rustic kitchen cabinets were crafted from reclaimed wood.

129

THINK GREEN

Recycling Room

Knowing what the recycling regulations and schedules are in your community will help you determine the best way to organize the cans, bottles, and other non-disposable items you use. Keep track of the quantity and types of recyclables your family generates between regular curbside pickups. Kitchen recycling storage units are available through cabinet and storage-product manufacturers.

office can be fitted with the leftovers and benefit from the added storage space.

If you are going to remove all your cabinets, don't automatically send them to the dump. Instead, arrange to donate them to a charitable organization such as Habitat for Humanity. Their crew can do the deconstruction work, keep the furnishings out of the landfill, and sell them at their ReStore. Proceeds from sales support their mission to end substandard housing. Work this out with the contractor ahead of time, because it will probably take more time to carefully remove them intact. You can sometimes receive a tax deduction for your donation. Another option is to search on the Internet for a deconstruction company that will carefully disassemble the kitchen in order to save components that can be recycled and sold.

Kitchen Appliances

Not only is the kitchen the hub of the home, it's also the area that uses the most energy. Kitchen appliances are used every day, and some—such as the refrigerator—run 24 hours no matter whether someone is in the room or not. There are many energy-efficient options available to help homeowners make a significant dent in their energy bills. These should be considered when redoing your kitchen, not only to save you money, but also to help reduce energy consumption and give the environment a break. Even if you don't replace all your appliances and lighting with energy-efficient models, just replacing one will make a big difference.

Government Guides

The government has implemented programs that set minimum efficiency levels for certain home appliances. The Federal Trade Commission (FTC) mandates mounting the EnergyGuide label on refrigerators, freezers, dishwashers, and many other household products. This label shows consumers the projected energy use and what the estimated yearly energy operating cost will be. The Energy Star program was created to help shoppers identify the most energy-efficient products on the market. If you buy an Energy Star product, you can be sure that it's a high-quality appliance that will ultimately help you save money due to lower operating costs over the course of its lifetime. In addition, local power companies often give customers

OPPOSITE LEFT The five different wood finishes in this kitchen blend into a warm, harmonious look.

OPPOSITE RIGHT Flea market silverware finds are stored and displayed for future use.

BELOW Shimmering glass tiles, a gooseneck kitchen faucet, and a mix of door and drawer knobs and pulls update the look of this kitchen.

ABOVE Straw, bamboo, and linen tabletop accessories add natural texture and tone to this dark wood table.

rebates if they replace their old appliances with energy-efficient models.

Refrigerators

Refrigerators have really evolved. Current models sport sleek good looks and smart features you could have barely imagined a decade ago. Even more important, their energy usage has dramatically improved. In most households, the refrigerator is the single biggest energy-consuming appliance. It's no wonder: the fridge runs nonstop. Also, the popular icemaker feature can increase energy use by 20 percent. Buying a more energy-efficient model will definitely reduce your electric bill and cut down on air pollution and global warming. In 2018, Energy Star's list of certified appliances included a top-freezer refrigerator model that uses less energy than a 60-watt light bulb. If your refrigerator is more than 10 years old and you upgrade to a newer Energy Star model, you could save more than $270 over the next 5 years on utility bills. You can get more details about individual units on the Energy Star website. (See the Resource Guide on page 208.)

Dishwashers

The good news about a dishwasher is that it uses less water than washing by hand. Most of the energy consumed by the dishwasher comes from heating the water. Over the past ten years, advanced technology in dishwashers enables the machines to adjust the cycle to optimize cleaning with minimal water. Make sure you buy a dishwasher with light, medium, and heavy wash settings and an energy-saving no-heat dry or air-dry setting. Energy Star certified dishwashers use less than half the energy of hand washing, and no pre-rinsing is needed—just scrape off food and load the dishes.

Cooking Appliances

Manufacturers of today's cooking equipment make it easier than ever to prepare fresh meals in short order. Some new ranges and ovens roast or bake foods in a fraction of conventional cooking times. Also,

LIVE WISE, LIVE WELL

Out with the Old

When your new refrigerator arrives, make sure you recycle your old one. Check with your community's public works department. They may pick up the old fridge for free or charge a small fee. Some retailers, also for a small fee, will pick up and dispose of your old refrigerator when they deliver the new one. Look into rebates from your local utility company — some offer cash incentives simply for letting them recycle your old energy-guzzling fridge.

LEFT Commercial-style refrigeration units are popular in today's high-end kitchens. This built-in unit blends seamlessly into the layout.

ABOVE The stainless-steel surfaces in this kitchen form a neutral background that highlights the warm wood and contemporary styling of the cabinets.

a suit-yourself approach allows you to customize these appliances according to your cooking style. You can now get a dual-fuel range that combines gas burners with an electric oven, or a separate cooktop featuring both gas and electric cooking elements. For two-cook kitchens, mini cooking stations—or "hubs"—can be configured as you wish, with one or two burners plus a steamer or grill, for example.

GAS COOKTOPS VERSUS ELECTRIC COOKTOPS

The use of gas or electric energy for your kitchen appliances is based on whether your neighborhood supplies gas service. Gas cooktops start up quickly, cook evenly, and are easy to control. Gas is somewhat more energy efficient, but not enough to make a big difference in your energy bill. The downside to using gas is that it releases unhealthy combustion byproducts into your home. You should always use a range hood that vents to the outdoors with a gas appliance. Fans that just recirculate air don't expel gases and odors to the outdoors.

Coil-style electric burners heat up quickly but cool slowly; however, they cost less to purchase. Ceramic cooktops heat up quickly, and their sleek glass surfaces are easy to clean. Halogen cooktops use tungsten halogen bulbs under a glass surface to generate

LEFT The range in this kitchen was chosen for its professional-style features, such as the six burners, griddle, and oversized ovens. A powerful exhaust system is necessary for this type of range.

heat. Magnetic induction cooktops provide the most energy efficiency. They convert electricity to magnetic currents that heat up only the cookware and the food. The main drawback is that these models are expensive and only work with cast iron, porcelain over cast iron, or stainless-steel cookware.

OVENS

Conventional gas and electric ovens cook via heated air. Many people prefer electric ovens because they provide a more even temperature

RIGHT A secondary food serving station lets family members prepare quick snacks and drinks away from the main cooking area.

than gas ovens. If you select a gas oven, take the same precautions as mentioned above with gas cooktops. Head off any potential air pollution from combustion byproducts by using a hooded system that's vented to the outside. Standard gas or electric ovens that are self-cleaning are more energy efficient because they have more insulation. However, if you use the self-cleaning feature more than once a month, you'll end up using more energy than you save from the extra insulation.

Electric convection ovens have one or more fans that circulate heated air around the food for faster, more even cooking and browning. They are becoming popular for the quality of their cooking and the decreased cooking time compared to a conventional oven. The use of a convection oven will reduce energy use by about one-third.

Microwave ovens use high-frequency radio waves to penetrate the food's surface and heat up water molecules inside the food. Energy consumption and cooking times for most foods are greatly reduced, especially for small portions and leftovers that need to be rewarmed. Microwave ovens use about two-thirds less energy than conventional types and may reduce air conditioning costs in the summer because they generate less heat.

ABOVE These wall ovens and adjacent microwave are a good choice for large families who entertain frequently.

RIGHT Ceramic-glass cooktops heat up quickly and clean easily. The large front burner can function as a 9 inch (23 centimeter) or 12 inch (30 centimeter) burner, depending on the size of the pot or pan.

Kitchen Ventilation

Ventilation systems are perhaps not as fun as top-of-the-line cooking equipment, but without one, your kitchen will harbor unwanted smells and your house may have increased air pollution and moisture levels. A hooded ventilation system installed directly over the cooking surface is the most effective way to expel combustion byproducts from gas cooking appliances, smoke, grease, and other nasty odors. The hood captures cooking air as it rises and a fan expels it outside through a duct. Make sure that the range hood is part of a vented system. Otherwise, it's just circulating odors and polluted air throughout the house. A kitchen range hood should be at least as wide as the cooking surface it will serve and mounted directly over it at a height of 18 to 30 inches (45 to 75 centimeters) above the burners. When shopping for an exhaust fan, look for a variable speed option that lets you use the lowest effective setting so your energy consumption can be reduced. Go to the Home Ventilating Institute's website, *www.hvi.org*, to see general guidelines on how to choose the best size fan for your needs.

BELOW Hidden under a decorative "mantel," this cooktop ventilation system is both a focal point and a powerhouse for removing smoke, moisture, and cooking odors.

Hoodless Downdraft Ventilation

Used often with island cooktops, downdraft ventilation forces the air above the burners through a filter, then out of the house via ductwork under the floor. It's not as effective as a hooded system, but it is better than a ductless fan.

Sinks and Faucets

What could be more basic to the modern kitchen than a sink and faucet? Yet in today's world, there's nothing basic about them. There are designs and finishes to suit any taste and budget. Far from being strictly utilitarian, sinks and faucets have evolved into highly decorative elements.

RIGHT This under-mounted porcelain-covered cast-iron sink pairs beautifully with the marble countertop.

Sinks

Sinks come in all sizes, shapes, and colors and are typically fabricated from enameled cast iron, stainless steel, solid stone, concrete, or a composite product, such as solid-surfacing material, acrylic, or a mixture of natural quartz or granite with resins. They may be contoured, beveled, brushed to a matte finish, or polished to a mirror finish. A popular trend is to include the largest sink you can accommodate within the confines of your space. Deep basins make it easier to deal with awkward, oversized items, such as large roasting pans and tall pots used for cooking pasta and soups. Shallow basin sinks are also available. These are useful when there is no other place to install the dishwasher but underneath the sink.

If you are interested in green design, the good news is that any of the materials mentioned above will hold up well for years—if not decades—with the right care. Enameled cast-iron sinks tend to discolor, but can be cleaned with nonabrasive cleanser.

Stainless steel sinks are a popular choice because they are relatively inexpensive, blend with contemporary décor, and are easy to maintain. They also have an eco-friendly edge because they're made with recycled content and can be recycled again at the end of their use. Avoid a sink with a gauge number higher than 18. The lower the gauge number, the thicker and heavier the sink; a higher number means thinner steel that can dent or scratch more easily. Look for a model made from a single sheet without any seams or rims.

ABOVE This shapely double sink is deep enough to handle large pots.

141

ABOVE LEFT A high-arched, satin nickel faucet can accommodate oversized pots and pans as well as tall flower vases.

ABOVE RIGHT This deck-mounted fitting in a burnished finish is a reproduction of a Victorian-era model.

Faucets

Faucets are no longer considered simply conduits for water. From sleek, European-inspired designs to graceful gooseneck shapes, today's selections add beauty as well as function to the kitchen. State-of-the-art faucet technology not only provides much more control over water use, but better performance and more extensive choices for finishes.

Most new faucets have built-in flow control devices that help make more efficient use of water. The aerator (the screw-on tip of the faucet) is what determines the flow rate for water. It mixes air into the stream of water and cuts usage without affecting water pressure. Most new kitchen faucets have a 2.2 gallon-per-minute (8.3 liter-per-minute) aerator. If you aren't changing faucets, it's very inexpensive to buy one of these new aerators and attach it to your old model. Buy one with a flow rate of 2.2 gallons (8.3 liters) per minute or less. Bring your old aerator and washer to the store when you buy a new one to make certain it will fit.

Water Filters

It's likely that your tap water is perfectly safe. However, many people worry about pollutants that might be in their water system. You can find out if there are any contaminants in your water by contacting your municipality and asking for a copy of their water-quality report.

LEFT Some faucets, such as this one, come with a built-in water filtering system.

If you have a private well, contact your local health department and ask for a list of well-water contaminants in your area.

Should you decide that you need a water-filtering system in your home, there are some things you should know. There are two basic categories of household water filters: point-of-entry systems, which treat water before it enters the house; and point-of-use units, which are installed at the fixture. Point-of-entry units are good if you have well water because sediments can shorten the life span of hot-water heaters and fixtures.

Point-of-use units can be installed under the sink, on the counter, or attached to the faucet itself. Before you buy one, check price, features, and the expected frequency and cost of filter replacement. The most common type is an activated carbon filter, which absorbs lead, chlorine byproducts, and other chemicals that affect odor and taste.

ABOVE A white china bowl heaped with crimson radishes provides a pop of bright, natural color in this neutral kitchen.

Also check for certification by NSF International, a nonprofit testing lab that certifies the efficiency of a filter in removing contaminants. You may also search for the Certified Products database on the Internet. Finally, if you live in an area with more serious pollution problems, consider a reverse-osmosis or distillation system.

Waste Disposal

When planning a new kitchen, make sure to set aside an area for a recycling center with bins for glass, plastic, metal, and paper. Try to put it in an easily accessible part of the kitchen so that family members will be more likely to use it. Most cabinets have add-on interior slide accessories that can accommodate trash bins specifically for recyclables. Garbage disposals are handy devices that grind up organic wastes and flush them down the drain. However, garbage disposals use up electricity and water and can also clog municipal waste systems. If you decide to purchase one, check local building codes to see if it's legal in your area. As far as a green kitchen goes, a better alternative would be to save your food scraps to make compost. Bins are available that keep out bugs and contain the scraps.

Kitchen Lighting

Whether you're remodeling an old kitchen or building a new one, abundant light should be high on the list of the features you will incorporate. Without it, a kitchen isn't pleasant, efficient, or safe. In fact, lack of light is one of the reasons homeowners decide to remodel. Because lighting a kitchen uses a lot of energy, make sure your choices are as energy-efficient as possible.

Using Natural Light

"Daylighting," an eco-design concept that focuses on incorporating an ideal amount of natural light into a room design, is a great way to decrease energy use and maximize visual comfort and productivity. This is particularly important in the kitchen because so many tasks are performed there—from cooking to reading to paying bills. Most architects, designers, and remodeling contractors can help you bring abundant natural light into your new kitchen and establish a connection with the outdoors. If you're starting from scratch, plan for the windows early in the process, while you are laying out the food

BELOW The large window over the sink provides abundant natural light in this kitchen and offers the chef a pleasant view while prepping and cooking.

preparation and dining zones. If you're remodeling, look for ways to enlarge existing windows or determine the best place to install new ones. You might also add windows or glass doors that overlook the garden or install a greenhouse window above the sink to supply sunshine and a spot to grow herbs year-round.

Skylights are another way to add more natural light to the kitchen. They are installed on the roof and are usually not reachable. Roof windows controlled by an electric wall switch or remote control device will let you open them to provide fresh air and ventilation. Make sure they're double glazed to minimize winter heat loss or summer heat gain.

Artificial Lighting

To create a warm, inviting, and functional kitchen, you will need artificial lighting as well as sources of natural light.

The most energy-efficient option is light-emitting diode bulbs (LEDs). Ninety percent of the energy used by standard incandescent bulbs produces heat rather than light. LEDs use about 70–90 percent less energy and last at least 15 times as long as traditional

 THINK GREEN

Safe Disposal of CFL Bulbs

Compact fluorescent lamps (CFLs) are also very economical and were the first type of bulb introduced as a transition away from energy-burning incandescents. One of the drawbacks of CFL bulbs is that they contain a small amount of mercury, a toxic metal that needs to be properly disposed of or recycled. LED bulbs contain no hazardous chemicals, and components can be recycled. Check with your local recycling program or a major home repair store to find out how to recycle both CFL and LED bulbs in your area. Or visit either *www.earth911.org* or *www.epa.gov/cfl* to find more information about hazardous waste collection in your area.

LEFT A dining table set for late afternoon tea will enjoy natural illumination from the candlelit chandelier.

incandescent bulbs. If possible, choose Energy Star–approved lamps and fixtures, because they have been proven to meet or exceed Environmental Protection Agency (EPA) standards for color and efficiency.

To find an LED that has the right amount of light, just choose one that's equivalent to the incandescent bulbs you've been using. Look for lumens rather than watts. LEDs produce varying shades of light, ranging from warmer tones to cooler tones. If you want a purer light that's more like natural daylight, choose one that's marketed as "cool white." Not all LEDs work with a dimmer mechanism, so be sure to check the packaging first if you're installing that kind of fixture. For spot or task lighting, choose LEDs with reflectors rather than a spiral bulb.

Bathrooms

Today's bathrooms are variously described as beautiful, luxurious, relaxing, and romantic. But let's not forget functional. The bathroom is a hardworking area that must be planned with careful attention to practical matters such as layout, safety, storage, durability, and maintenance. The space is often small, yet it must be able to accommodate a variety of large features. When planning the layout, try angling a sink or shower unit in a corner to free up some floor space. Also, consider installing a pocket door that slides into the wall to create more useable space. You can also make your bathroom feel roomier by bringing in natural light with a skylight or light tube, or by replacing a standard window with several small casement or clerestory units that can be installed high on the wall to maintain privacy.

The bathroom is a big water and energy guzzler. Toilets account for around 30 percent of residential water consumption, and showers account for about 37 percent of your household's hot-water usage. Add onto that the energy used by your water heater to maintain the perfect temperature for that long, luxurious bath, and you've got a major drain on energy resources. Reducing your water consumption has far-reaching benefits. Not only does it allow rivers and streams to maintain adequate water levels, but it also reduces the need to develop new water treatment facilities and water storage. Luckily, there are many products on the market today that are both beautiful and help reduce your water usage and expenditures.

To find water-efficient products and services more easily, the EPA has initiated the WaterSense program, designed to protect the water supply by promoting efficient products and services. Products that

LEFT A lav console made of clear glass enhances light flow and creates an airy, open feeling in this small bathroom.

have been shown to meet stringent standards backed up by independent testing and certification are given the WaterSense label. Generally speaking, WaterSense-labeled products are 20 percent more efficient than their standard counterparts. The WaterSense program encourages water conservation behaviors and provides consumers with the assurance that they are buying efficient and high-performance products.

Tubs

The possibilities for tubs are endless. They include soakers, tubs for two, spas for four, oval, square, and rounded shapes, whirlpools, tubs set into platforms, and tubs you step down into to enter.

ABOVE Treasures from the sea make perfect natural accessories for the bathroom.

RIGHT Honey-hued ceramic tiles, rich wood, and a burnished animal hide rug create a striking look in this master bathroom.

LIVE WISE, LIVE WELL

Waste Not, Want Not

An easy way to cut down on water use is to take shorter showers. It's simple to calculate: if your shower head sprays out 2.5 gallons (9.5 liters) of water per minute and you spend two minutes less in the shower, you'll save 5 gallons (19 liters) of water. A year's worth of daily showers would use 1,825 fewer gallons (6,900 fewer liters) of water.

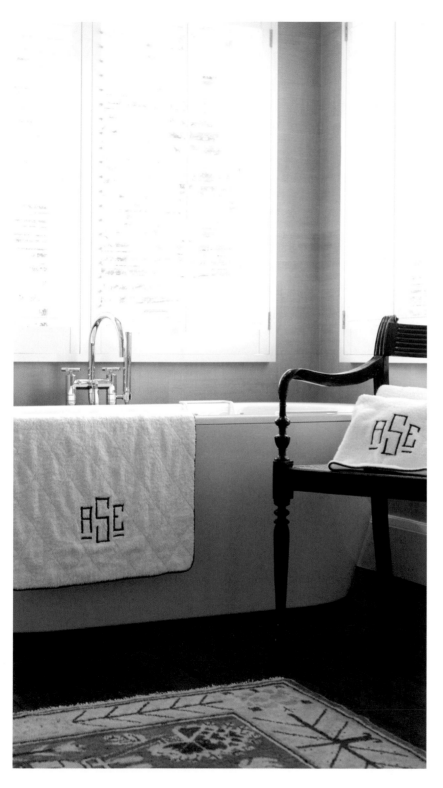

LEFT The simple design of this deep soaking tub marries well with traditional or contemporary décor.

Before you buy, consider how often you really plan to use the tub. When designing your bathroom, decide whether freestanding or built-in equipment is best for your space. A freestanding tub and shower can provide a focal point in a large bathroom. A built-in tub that's attached to the wall and floor will probably be the best use of space in a small room.

Tubs can be constructed from various materials, including:

- **Enameled cast-iron** tubs will endure as long as your house stands. However, they are heavy and therefore not recommended for a large soaking tub or spa.
- **Porcelain on steel (POS)** is a very common bathtub material. POS is relatively light, moderately priced, and resists corrosion and abrasion. However, this material tends to rust if the porcelain chips or cracks.
- **Acrylic** tubs are lighter in weight than other materials, making them a popular choice for whirlpool baths and large soaking tubs. Acrylic can wear and scratch over time, but scratches can often be buffed out. Acrylic is resistant to most chemicals.
- **Fiberglass** tubs are the least expensive option. Although it can be repaired fairly easily, fiberglass is not a highly durable product and may scratch and fade over time.

Showers

The ideal shower should be both invigorating and cleansing. Many styles of showerheads will deliver water, but water efficiency should be at the top of the list of your concerns when making your selection. Look for an efficient one with a low flow rate of less than 2 gallons (7.6 liters) per minute (gpm), which earns the WaterSense seal of approval. Before federal guidelines were established in 1994, older models used up to 5 gallons (19 liters) per minute. Even at 2 gpm (7.6 liters per minute) or less, there are still a wide variety of spray patterns and options such as pulsing or soft rain sprays.

There are two basic types of low-flow showerheads:

- **Aerating heads** are the most popular low-flow type. They work by incorporating air into the water to form a misty spray. Because air cools faster than water, sometimes the water will feel a bit cooler, especially toward the floor of the shower.
- **Non-aerating** or **laminar flow heads** form individual streams rather than mixing air with water. This type is good for humid climates because they don't create as much steam as an aerating head. Look for showerheads with the WaterSense label.

OPPOSITE This master bathroom features a spa-like soaking tub and a separate shower area for quick cleaning.

THINK GREEN

Green T.P.

When you're flushing, be sure to use recycled toilet paper. Several options are available that are just as soft as the regular stuff. You'll help save trees and reduce environmental pollution.

BELOW WaterSense-labeled toilets use 20 percent less than the federal standard; look for the label when shopping for a toilet.

Toilets

There are many new toilet features on the market today. Vitreous china is still the most popular material used for toilets, but there's a wide range of colors and styles to suit any décor. If your taste is contemporary, select a European-inspired, elongated bowl. Though toilet sizes vary somewhat among manufacturers, an elongated bowl will extend about 2 inches (5 centimeters) more into the room than a standard version. The typical height of a toilet seat is 15 inches (38 centimeters), but some come as high as 18 inches (45 centimeters), which can accommodate taller family members. Scaled-down toilets are available for apartments, powder rooms, and small bathrooms tucked under a stairwell or converted from a closet.

One of the major water guzzlers in the home is toilet flushing. If your home was built before 1992 and you haven't replaced the toilet, you could benefit from installing one of the new high-efficiency toilets. These toilets conform to the government's low-flush standard, which mandates that no more than 1.6 gallons (6 liters) of water be used per flush. (Older models used between 3.5 gallons [13 liters] and a whopping 6 gallons [22.7 liters] per flush.) When shopping for a new toilet, look for the WaterSense label, which guarantees that the toilet uses no more than 1.28 gallons (4.8 liters) per flush.

Dual-flush toilets are also excellent for reducing water usage. Although they've been around for years, they've recently become more widely available. Dual-flush toilets have a simple, two-option flushing system. A partial flush releases a small volume (about 0.8 gallons [3 liters]) of water for flushing liquid and paper waste; the full flush releases a larger volume (around 1.6 gallons [6 liters]) for solid waste. This gives the user the ability to reduce water consumption according to waste. Dual-flush toilets use about 20 percent less water than standard toilets.

Sinks

You may find it practically impossible to select one lavatory over another because they come in so many sizes, shapes, styles, and colors. Sensuous curves, sculpted bowls, and beautiful, durable finishes can make these everyday objects works of art—and an important element in your bathroom's overall design. Vitreous china, enameled steel, stone and concrete, or stainless steel are all natural materials and come in a wide variety of styles. They are also long-lasting and environmentally friendly. A sink can be a freestanding pedestal, or it can be mounted to the wall or installed as part of a vanity top.

There are attractive, shapely sinks in every price range. If you will do anything at the sink besides washing up and brushing your teeth, consider your choice of design and size carefully before you buy. Something that is too shallow, for example, may not be practical for rinsing hair or washing lingerie. A pedestal sink may be pretty, but lacks surface space for grooming or shaving. This style might work best in a powder room.

RIGHT Undermounted sinks blend the lav almost seamlessly into the countertop for a sleek, contemporary look. Added bonus: it makes cleaning easier.

Faucets and Other Fittings

Like showers, faucets are no longer just conduits for water. Today's faucet technology gives you much more control over your water flow. For example, you can program some faucets to create a pulsating effect, or select the gentler rhythm of a babbling brook or a cascading waterfall. You can even preset water temperature so that water never gets hotter than you like, which is a plus for protecting children, the disabled, or the elderly from scalding.

The bathroom sink faucet, also controlled by government standards, must use 2.2 gallons (8.3 liters) per minute or less. Many faucets have aerators that restrict water flow to as little as 1.0 gpm (3.8 liters per minute). Look for the WaterSense label to be sure that your faucet is efficient. If you aren't going to buy a new faucet, get better energy savings on your old one by installing an aerator to reduce the flow rate. Some aerators have a flip switch to turn the faucet on and off without losing your water temperature.

To ensure a quality product, inquire about the materials used inside the faucet. The best choices are solid brass or a brass base metal, which are resistant to corrosion. Avoid plastic—it won't hold up. Inquire about the faucet's valves, too. Many faucets come with

ABOVE This deck-mounted widespread faucet has a high-arc spout that reaches well into the basin.

a washerless ceramic or nylon cartridge that lasts longer and is less prone to leaks. Ceramic is the better choice. Select finishes according to your taste and other elements in the room that you may wish to coordinate with the fittings. Finishes, such as chrome, polished brass, pewter, nickel, and bronze, enhance natural decorating schemes.

There are three basic faucet types:

- **Center set faucets** have two separate valves for hot and cold water connected by a center spout.
- **Widespread faucets** feature a spout with separate hot- and cold-water valves. All of the parts appear to be completely separate pieces.
- **Single-lever faucets** have a spout and a single lever in one piece for use with one hand.

Remember function when selecting your faucet. Decorative handles are charming, but they can be difficult to grasp for the elderly, the disabled, or the very young. Levers and wrist blades make more sense in these cases. If you prefer a single-lever faucet, install one with a hot-water safety valve.

BELOW Mirrors and white walls and cabinetry reflect light so this bathroom has plenty of illumination.

Bathrooms: Light and Air

Many designers recommend a layered approach to lighting in today's bathroom. Start with as much daylight as possible through a window or skylight that also provides necessary ventilation. Then add a dose of the right combination of artificial lighting to enhance the sunshine and illuminate the room at night.

Natural and Artificial Light

Whether you are remodeling an old bathroom or building a new one, pay attention to the variety of options you have for incorporating windows. Your selection should be based on what looks best with the rest of the room, of course, but don't forget to consider energy efficiency. Today's windows and skylights have better seals than older versions. Multiple panes, low-emissivity (low-E) coatings, and gas-filled spaces between panes can reduce unwanted heat loss and gain. Solar tubes that

run from the roof to the ceiling also provide abundant natural light without much energy loss. When shopping, always consider your climate and the window's orientation.

You'll also need good artificial light to provide adequate illumination and increase the safety of the room. In the bathroom, you'll not only need general lighting for the whole room, but also separate task fixtures for grooming. For your face to look good in the mirror, light should come from both sides, radiating from the middle of your face (about 60 to 66 inches [152 to 167 centimeters] from the floor for most adults). LED or CFL bulbs offer the best energy efficiency. They cast a diffuse, shadowless light that is great for general illumination. Another option, especially for recessed or indirect lights, is halogen lighting. It offers as much light as incandescent bulbs but uses half the power. You can also save energy if you wire different lights to separate switches so you only have to turn on the light you need.

ABOVE A large window has translucent shades to let in filtered light, yet still provide privacy in this bathroom.

Abundant natural light is the most beautiful enhancement to your bathroom

Ventilation

It's very important that the bathroom is well-ventilated because all of the moisture generated there can lead to mold and mildew. In fact, most local building codes require fans in bathrooms that don't have windows. Even if you do have access to natural ventilation, there are times when you won't want to keep a window open. When you purchase a ventilating system, search out those that have an Energy Star rating. This guarantees a high energy-efficiency rating and top performance.

RIGHT A claw-foot tub is centered in front of a bank of windows so it can receive daylight and adequate ventilation.

 LIVE WISE, LIVE WELL

Reduce Your Carbon Footprint

- Don't let the water run when brushing your teeth, shaving, or washing.
- Repair leaky fixtures and install low-flow faucets and showerheads.
- Buy toilet paper and other paper products made from recycled material.

LEFT While most windows provide ventilation, an Energy Star–rated exhaust fan is more effective, especially in winter when windows stay closed.

ABOVE Sea sponges and other natural accessories enhance an eco-friendly design.

There are three types of bathroom ventilation systems:

- **Recirculating fans** move the air around in the room. Although they do not vent to the outdoors, they help to dispel some of the moisture that has accumulated on surfaces during bathing.
- **Ducted systems** discharge humidity in the bathroom by removing moist, stale air and odors and venting them through ductwork to the outdoors. Some of the latest offerings include remote-operated units, built-in lighting, heaters, multiple speeds, silent operation, and automatic-on features triggered by a humidity sensor.
- **Room exhaust fans** consist of separate exhaust fans mounted on the ceiling or outer wall of a new bathroom. The fan must be connected to the outside via a vent cap on the roof or sidewall. To effectively remove moisture and odors from the bathroom, you need to match the fan capacity to the room's dimensions. The Home Ventilating Institute offers guidelines for ventilating large and small bathrooms. (See the Resource Guide on page 208.) Noise is another issue when shopping for exhaust fans. Fan noise is rated in sones. The quietest bathroom exhaust fans measure approximately one sone—about the level of a refrigerator fan.

Sometimes, more than one fan is recommended for efficient venting, especially in large bathrooms. Of course, check with your local building department about codes that may stipulate where to install bathroom fans. If possible, include a fan in the toilet area, near the shower, and over the bathtub.

Storage for the Bathroom

Storage is a key issue in any bathroom, no matter what the size. To obtain the right amount for your needs, you'll have to thoroughly analyze your space and prioritize what items you must have handy, as well as any extras you'd appreciate having nearby. With clever planning, it's possible for even a tiny bathroom to accommodate spare rolls of toilet paper, additional bars of soap, hairstyling products, shaving accessories, and a stack of clean towels—as long as you consider storage issues in the earliest stage of your design project.

RILEY

LEFT Hooks on the back of the door provide a very convenient place for bathrobe or towel storage. Plastic or coated-metal hooks are best for use in damp spaces.

It's likely that you'll want at least a vanity and medicine cabinet in your new bathroom. Like fixtures and fittings, these make a big impact on how the new space will look as well as how it will function.

Vanities

There are many creative ways to approach the vanity. One is to treat it as a decorative receptacle for a drop-in sink with just a countertop and legs and no attached cabinetry. If you can sacrifice the storage a cabinet provides, this option will add drama to your design, especially if the countertop is outfitted with handsome tile, stone, or colored concrete. However, if you're limited by space and have to make the most of every inch, a vanity cabinet that features drawers and shelves is the wisest choice.

Whether you want stock, semicustom, or custom cabinets, choose ones that are made of FSC-certified wood with wood interiors. If these are beyond your budget, search for cabinets that have cores and frames made out of materials that are free of urea-formaldehyde. If formaldehyde-free cabinets aren't an option, see if you can arrange to have the cabinets delivered a few weeks ahead of time, and air them out in a well-ventilated garage. The Kitchen Cabinet Manufacturers Association has launched an Environmental Stewardship Program to recommend cabinets that have been made in an environmentally responsible manner.

A popular and eco-friendly option is to retrofit a piece of fine wood furniture, such as an antique chest, with a sink, reproduction fittings, and an elegant countertop. The wood surfaces should be sealed with a low-VOC protective coating that resists water and mildew. If you don't have the right piece of old furniture but want the same look, check out the new cabinet styles offered by many manufacturers today.

ABOVE Mementos from the beach bring personalized touches and a link to nature in the bathroom.

OPPOSITE This handsome custom vanity provides shelf and drawer storage to keep towels, toiletries, and grooming appliances neatly organized.

CHAPTER 6

Open to Nature

Designing around the great outdoors

A room filled with natural light and verdant views can lift your spirits and enhance your sense of well-being. Morning sunshine in a bedroom or breakfast nook eases you gently into the day. In warmer seasons and climates, it's wonderful to spend as much time as possible in nature, dining on a leafy patio or relaxing by an outdoor fireplace.

LIGHT-FILLED PLACES CAN ACT AS pleasant transitions that link the interior of your home to the outdoors. A garden room connecting a kitchen to a patio is a perfect breakfast area that provides a wonderful wake-up call, no matter what the season. A sunroom overlooking the backyard makes an excellent sitting room or play area. A few well-situated, large windows can blur the line between the interior of your house and the landscape beyond. Conservatories, sunrooms, and windows—all can link a home to the beauty of nature.

OPPOSITE A teak pedestal table and cushioned chairs makes eating outdoors as comfortable as dining inside. The generous curtain treatment frames the view and protects the eating area.

Windows

Windows play an important role in providing comfort in your home. They control the amount of light and air that enters the house. Rooms that are bright and sunny project a sense of energy and well-being. You want to spend time there because it's easier to do your daily tasks in a room filled with natural light. The flow of light from windows also influences your decorating decisions. The quality and quantity of available light can enhance or detract from colors that you choose for your rooms. White, for instance, will look different depending on what kind of light fills the room: it could appear gray in a room with a dim northern exposure, golden in a room with late-day sun, or bright white in a room that's sunny all day. In a very sunny room, wood surfaces that absorb light will be easier to live with than glossy granite ones that reflect light.

Windows and Energy Efficiency

Windows can directly affect your energy bills. Choosing energy-efficient windows ensures that heat doesn't escape from your house

BELOW Floor-to-ceiling windows flood this bedroom with light. With this expanse of glass, it's important that windows are energy efficient to keep utility bills low.

in the winter; in summer, they prevent hot air from entering and air-conditioned air from leaking outside. This way, heating and cooling bills can be substantially reduced. Relying on natural light for daily activities instead of switching on a lamp will also affect your electric bill. Before installing new windows, check with your local utility company. It may offer information as well as rebates on energy-efficient products. New windows may be a big investment, but it pays to buy the best you can afford.

Choosing Green Windows

Before you invest in new windows, arm yourself with the latest information. Be aware that the number of panes in a window affects its energy efficiency. Single-pane units are the least efficient. Double- or triple-pane windows consist of multiple layers of glass with inert gases, such as argon or krypton, filling the air space to reduce heat transfer and provide better sound insulation. Many window manufacturers also offer low-emissivity (low-E) coatings. Installed in the space of a double-pane window, they aren't visible to the eye. These coatings work by reflecting infrared light to keep heat inside in winter and outside in summer. They also reflect damaging ultraviolet light to keep furniture, fabrics, and artwork from fading. There are different types of low-E coatings for high, moderate, and low solar gain. (For a listing of websites that offer information on various energy-efficient home products, see the Resource Guide on page 208.) Also check for any federal tax credits or local utility rebates for installing energy-efficient windows.

Look for windows and skylights rated by the National Fenestration Rating Council (NFRC). The sticker on the product will list the U-factor and the solar heat gain coefficient (SHGC) of the windows. The U-factor measures how much heat flows through the window. The lower the U-factor, the better insulated the window. SHGC measures how well the window blocks heat from the sun. Always look for Energy Star products. The Energy Star website provides information on the U-factor and SHGC that is appropriate for your climate zone. Be sure that your windows are installed by a trained professional following the manufacturer's guidelines.

Window Frames

Residential window frames and sashes are made of wood, vinyl, fiberglass, or aluminum. While wood windows are an environmentally preferable material, they require upkeep because

RIGHT Light tones on the walls, sofa, and floor intensify the daylight by reflecting the light streaming in from the large windows.

exposure to the elements can cause deterioration. Vinyl-clad wood windows are a sensible, low-maintenance option because they resist corrosion and denting, offer excellent insulation, and don't require painting or protective coatings. Vinyl windows are available with wood cladding on the interior. Inexpensive aluminum windows offer the lowest-quality insulation.

LEFT An L-shaped banquette is completely surrounded by windows to give the feeling of eating outdoors.

ABOVE This dining room is usually flooded with light, but Roman shades can be pulled down at night or to prevent glare.

Window Types

There are several basic window styles. Fixed windows cannot be opened and are often used in combination with operable windows. Double-hung windows are the most common of the operable types; they have two sashes that move up and down, which means that only half of the window can be open at any one time. Casement windows are hinged vertically to swing in or out in a door-like manner; they are operated by a crank. Awning windows are hinged horizontally, with narrow strips of glass that are opened in a louver-like fashion by operating a crank. Sliding windows have top and bottom tracks along which the sash moves sideways.

Windows and Natural Ventilation

After the 1970s, new homes were tightly sealed to improve energy efficiency. It is now known that this type of construction has a

LEFT French doors open to provide natural light and ventilation throughout this house.

THINK GREEN

Get a Solar Boost

If you have a sunroom or enclosed porch with a southern exposure, it can be used to collect tremendous amounts of heat. Use fans or natural convection to move air through a doorway from solar-warmed rooms to adjacent interior spaces. Just be sure to provide an opening for return air, such as a vent or an open window between the sunroom and the house, to ensure good air movement.

RIGHT Fresh-cut flowers instantly brighten a room by literally bringing nature indoors.

downside. Because you spend nearly 90 percent of your time indoors, you're more prone to be affected by air pollution from common household materials, such as cabinets, stoves, and carpets. If you're installing new windows, make sure to choose operable types so that you can naturally ventilate your home. This is especially important in kitchens, bathrooms, and laundry rooms.

Other Links to the Outdoors

Study the flow of light in your home. What rooms get the cool northern light and the evening shadows? How many windows are in each room? How large are the windows? You can better utilize the existing light if you match the use of the room to the quality of its light. Rooms with lots of sunlight should be reserved for family rooms or kids' playrooms that get a lot of daytime activity; darker spaces are better suited to a media room or study. Windows can also affect the location of furniture. If there's a beautiful picture window, make it a focal point of your room design.

LEFT Positioning tables and chairs next to windows provides a generous amount of natural light for reading and relaxing during the day.

RIGHT Because this room has wonderful light, the homeowners chose it for dining during daylight hours.

Daylighting, a term that describes one of the most popular tenets of energy-conscious home design, is simply the practice of using natural light to illuminate rooms during the day. You don't need to turn as many lights on, so you save on electricity bills. This can be accomplished through smart window design and location. Below are some special types of windows that can increase your natural light.

- **Skylights** and **roof windows** are installed on rooftops to bring light into the home. You should follow the same standards of energy efficiency as regular windows when shopping: look for double glazing, because these units tend to lose large amounts of energy through the glass in cold weather. Also, use these windows sparingly in warm climates because they can move significant amounts of heat into the house. You might consider a mechanized shade to control heat buildup during periods of high temperatures.
- **Tubular daylighting devices** run from the roof through the attic into the ceiling of a room. They send light down to a diffusing lens that's positioned on the ceiling. They are particularly adept at brightening up areas that wouldn't get a lot of natural light, such as bathrooms, hallways, or closets. Because they decrease the need for electric lighting, tubular daylights add to energy savings. Be sure that tubes are made of insulating material and wrapped in insulation to cut down on heat loss or gain.
- **Clerestory windows** consist of small, horizontal panes set on a wall close to the ceiling. These windows bring in added natural light. They should be made of double-pane glass and be operable so they can be opened in summer for ventilation.

Patio Doors

Patio and folding doors are the transition between your house and the outdoors. They afford you with a view of your deck or yard and come in a variety of configurations. Choose the widest door that will fit your plan.

There are two main categories of patio doors from which to choose: sliders (also called gliders) and hinged. Sliders save space because there is no need to accommodate door swing. If you go for a slider, invest in a quality unit with a secure locking system. A sticking door quickly becomes tiresome, so look for heavy-duty sills and stainless-steel or nylon ball-bearing rollers. Consider a unit with a sliding screen that automatically closes behind you so that you're not constantly asking kids to close the screen door. Today's sliding patio doors are available with wide stiles and rails that mimic the look of

ABOVE These hinged patio doors open inward so they don't interfere with traffic on the narrow deck area outside.

LIVE WISE, LIVE WELL

Decorating to Increase Natural Light

If you're not able to invest in new windows at the moment, some decorating tricks can help you increase the amount of light in your home.

- Put up window treatments that maximize light. Install mini blinds or louvered shutters. When opened, they direct light into a space; when closed, they block out excess heat.
- Install curtain rods above and beyond the sides and top of windows so you can pull the curtains back enough to expose the entire glass. This will make a big difference in the amount of sunshine that comes inside.
- Use sheer, open weave, or muslin fabrics to break up light at windows. They gently diffuse light into rooms while cutting down the glare.
- Decorate with whites, off-whites, or pale tones of yellow, blue, green, or gray. They reflect light across surfaces and make rooms glow. Put in light-color flooring near windows to bounce daylight into rooms. Light-color furniture and other flat surfaces and mirrors near windows will also transfer light into a space.

French doors. Extra-wide, three- and four-panel sliders are great for opening up your view.

There are several types of hinged patio doors. The simplest is a single-panel glass door. You can also order a two-panel hinged door with one or two operating panels. With one operating panel you will have to decide which panel you want to be stationary. Triple-panel doors are also available. Doors can be ordered to swing in or out. In addition, they can be hinged on the right or left side. You have lots of options, so think them through carefully with a catalog in hand to avoid mistakes. Avoid choosing a door configuration that will interfere with traffic or furniture, such as an out-swinging door that blocks access to deck stairs or an in-swinging door that cramps the seating for your kitchen table.

Screen doors complicate matters further. Double patio doors with a single out-swinging door, for example, may give you more space inside, but are often paired with a sliding screen on the inside. You may not want the screen frame blocking the wood frame of your new, expensive patio door. An in-swinging version of the same door typically comes with a sliding screen on the outside. Double patio doors with two in-swinging doors, however, will require double out-swinging screen doors or a single out-swinging screen door and one fixed-screen panel.

Folding Walls

Consider maximizing the interaction between inside and outside with a folding-wall system. These units go beyond multiple-panel doors by running the entire length of the wall, with no obstruction to the outside when they are opened. These dramatic openings are dynamic yet practical, making the outdoor space part of your kitchen, dining area, or even your bedroom.

There are several types of folding walls, including aluminum, wood with exterior aluminum cladding, and all-wood. There is even an all-glass option with no rails or stiles.

Mechanically speaking, door panels slide along a top-hung or floor-mounted track and stack separately or fold at hinges. If you live in an area subject to hurricanes, check to be sure your folding-wall manufacturer has a hurricane-approved system. Keep insects out using a roll-down screen or one that is pleated and slides.

Installing a folding-wall system is not a weekend do-it-yourself project. Use professional help to ensure that the opening is properly supported and operates smoothly.

LIVE WISE, LIVE WELL

Bring the Outdoors Inside

Looking for a way to add a garden room or sunroom without literally adding a new structure? Is there a small room in your house on an outside wall that serves no real purpose? Replace outside walls with glass, or install a bank of windows. Other ways to transform a stuffy, dark space into a sunny nook include enlarging existing windows, substituting sliding-glass or French doors, or adding a skylight. Ask an expert before planning changes that may affect structural elements in your home.

RIGHT Folding walls can be pulled back to make the outdoor space part of the living room area.

Eco-Shopping for Doors

Door designs are moving toward more glass today. Sidelights, stationary panels, and transoms combine to offer panoramic views. With that much exposure, energy efficiency is vital. Look for Energy Star–qualified products and check for ratings with the National Fenestration Rating Council (NFRC). Buying energy-efficient doors may entitle you to tax benefits. Lower your maintenance with doors that are clad with aluminum on the exterior. There are many stylish options, but views of your deck or patio will be the most attractive feature of them all.

Garden Rooms and Conservatories

Conservatories, sunrooms, and garden rooms can open your eyes and senses to the world outside. They provide living and entertaining space in the warm months and can add to the flow of fresh air throughout the home. In the winter months, they block the drafts from outside and absorb solar heat, which they can pass to the rest of the home.

ABOVE This window wall runs the entire length of the room. The outdoors can be accessed by French doors in the center.

LIVE WISE, LIVE WELL

Zone Heating

Keeping unused areas of your home cool while warming the spaces you're using will conserve large amounts of energy. The best time to install zone heating is when you're building a new house. Consider a hydronic (water- or steam-based) system. This will work especially well with radiant-heat floors.

Conservatories

Traditionally glass and metal structures primarily used to grow plants indoors, conservatories are enjoying a renewed popularity, thanks in part to improved technology. Insulated windows and more efficient heating and cooling make the addition of a conservatory to your home an attractive and affordable option. Most companies that build conservatories offer recommendations on the best location, style, and materials to suit your home. Before undertaking a project, check zoning and permit requirements. You should also know which energy-efficient window would be appropriate for your climate. Separate the structure from your living area with double-pane windows and doors to save on energy bills.

Sunrooms

While a conservatory is usually an all-glass structure that may be separate from the house, a sunroom generally shares the roofline of the house and has one or more walls made of windows. Sunrooms original to many older homes are not insulated, making them too cold for year-round use in all but the most southern climates. Replacing drafty windows with energy-efficient units updates the look of the sunroom and increases its comfort. Look for high-quality windows and doors with an Energy Star rating.

BELOW Sunrooms are the perfect place for favorite natural elements, such as a rock collection or a lush indoor garden.

Orienting Your Room

In general, think about how you want to use a sunny indoor space. For all uses but growing tropical plants, a conservatory with a southern exposure—which gets strong sunlight all day—would be too hot, especially during the summer. You will need ceiling fans or air conditioning and adjustable window coverings if you plan to do much living in that room. Facing west, the room will be more moderate in temperature, except in the late afternoon, the sunniest time of day for this location. If the room faces east, the brightest, cheeriest hours are in the early morning. Avoid locating your conservatory on the north side of the house. It won't get

any direct sunlight and it may even be too cold to use most of the year.

Ideas for Creating Indoor Garden-Room Style

The indoor garden room has the advantage of protection from the elements, much like a covered porch or patio. This makes your indoor garden retreat the perfect spot to put furniture made from natural materials: wicker or rattan chaises and chairs, a sisal or hooked rug, and accessories with a garden theme. Plus, these furnishings are lightweight so you can easily move them back and forth between the house and garden—further blurring the boundaries between indoors and outdoors. Other tips include:

- Try to use as many recycled materials as you can. Keep your eyes open at secondhand stores and tag sales for antique wicker or wire plant stands. Use rattan or twig furniture for rustic style.
- Don't forget interesting architectural elements. Bring in a stone statue. Use a section of substantial molding as a shelf. Plant trailing ivy in large metal or stone urns.

ABOVE A modern indoor/ outdoor room invites visitors to recline on its rattan and metal chaise lounges; one of the perks of an outdoor room is the opportunity to sip cocktails while enjoying the sunshine, park-like views, and gentle breezes.

- Include anything bird related, such as beautiful birdcages, a birdbath, framed prints of exotic birds, or a collection of birds' nests.
- Add plants. A sunroom can extend the gardening season even in the coldest climates, as well as provide a place to cultivate delicate specimens that require a controlled environment.

ABOVE A garden room provides a spot for everyone in the house to enjoy the warmth of the sun.

OPPOSITE Today's energy-efficient window glazing technology means that sunrooms like this one may be used year-round—whatever the weather.

Porches, Decks, and Patios

Before you decorate your outdoor space, there are a few things to consider. Is the space in front of or on the side of the house? How does it look from the inside of the house? Consider the scale of the furnishings. Indoor/outdoor furniture comes in a variety of sizes and styles; some are sleek and space-saving, others designed to visually fill up an area. Plan outdoor furnishings so that they augment a good view instead of blocking it. Once you have a style in mind, develop a plan that defines the function of the space.

Special Considerations

When deciding what type of furniture to buy and where to place it, factor in traffic patterns. Note the pathways into and out of the house. Take into account the swing of each door—you cannot place furniture

ABOVE The furniture in this outdoor living area was arranged in a conversation group positioned to make the most of the breathtaking view.

in those spaces. Arrange furniture so that conversation areas are not interrupted by traffic to and from the house. For instance, a common problem is a porch with a central door and a stepped entrance directly opposite the door. Rather than arranging furniture in one big grouping, create smaller areas at each end of the porch.

Also consider all the seasons that you'll use the space. For example, decide whether you want to add curtains to block chill winds during the winter months.

Plan an outdoor furniture arrangement to augment a spectacular view

Furnish with Care

There are many styles and materials of outdoor furniture from which to choose. You can select Adirondack-style seating, twig or wicker furniture, teak, metal, and many other materials. A word of caution: some furniture may not stand up to extremes in weather.

Check warranties and read directions on the furniture for care and maintenance. Then match your choices to the possible weather exposure. Choose new furniture made from recycled materials or secondhand furniture when possible. Someone else's castoffs can be freshened and given new life as garden décor. It will only add character to your outdoor space.

Natural Materials

Wood: The best choices are naturally weather-resistant woods, such as cypress, cedar, teak, or redwood. They require little upkeep, don't need staining or preservative coatings, and develop a beautiful patina after a season in the outdoors. Look for furniture with joints that are secured with both glue and screws to ensure the longevity and stability of the piece. Just like any other wood furniture, make sure it has eco-integrity by checking for the FSC label when purchasing. Better yet, save a tree and search antique stores for any good secondhand furniture that already has the patina of age. Make sure any finishes applied to wood have low VOC levels.

BELOW A classic conversation grouping provides the comfort of a living room while enjoying an alfresco dinner.

    Wicker, bamboo, and rattan: While furniture made out of these materials can make the perfect transition between the exterior and

interior of a home, they are susceptible to the elements and should be used only if the location is protected. Synthetic wicker look-alikes resemble the real thing and are reasonably resistant to sun and rain. Special finishes are available for wicker that will give it more weather resistance, but care should be taken to make sure they have low VOC levels.

Iron: For traditionalists, nothing beats classic wrought iron. Both cast and wrought iron will rust unless treated with special rust-inhibiting paint over the years. A good going over with a wire brush and a couple of coats of low-VOC enamel paint work wonders. Its weight makes iron a good choice for windy areas, but it is heavy and difficult to rearrange.

Porches

Porches fell out of favor in the latter half of the twentieth century due in part to modern architecture and the advent of air conditioning. Today more builders are adding porches to houses as homebuyers seek more traditional types of homes. They are an important architectural feature and add delightful living and entertaining space.

FRONT PORCHES

A well-designed porch complements the architecture of the house and serves as a visual and physical transition between indoors and outdoors. The most basic front porch consists of a few steps leading to a small landing, typically protected by an overhang. The essence of porch living is relaxation, and the only basic furnishing requirement is a perfect place to sit—whether it's a classic wooden rocker, a romantic two-person swing, or a comfy wicker chair. Whatever else you add depends on your lifestyle. If your front porch is the place where packages and mail are delivered, you'll need a table or basket to receive them. If it becomes the summer family room, include tables and storage accommodations in your plan. Porch décor should complement the interior style and color scheme of your home.

ENCLOSED PORCHES

A screened-in porch offers an old-fashioned appeal along with the benefit of bug-free comfort. This makes it an ideal spot for visiting, reading, late dining—even sleeping when the weather is hot. Usually located on the side or the back of the house, a screened-in porch also offers more privacy than one that is open, so the design can be intimate and informal.

If the addition of a new structure isn't possible, consider adding screens or windows to an existing porch. This is a relatively

OPPOSITE This woven bamboo chair and ottoman fit naturally next to the rough stone wall of the house.

RIGHT A second-story porch allows the homeowners to enjoy a bird's-eye view of the street below.

inexpensive way to maximize your living area. If insects prevent you from enjoying your deck or patio, add a roof or overhang to cover the area and enclose the sides. Because this will affect the roofline of your house, consult with an architect before embarking on this project.

DECORATING YOUR PORCH

Pillows, upholstery, slipcovers, shades and blinds, lighting, flooring, and rugs all make your outdoor room lush and comfortable. The materials you can use depend on how rigorous the weather is on the furnishings. In a relatively dry, hot climate, for instance, sun resistance is the quality you want most, while mildew resistance is less essential.

LEFT A front porch with its rocking chairs facing the street and a sky blue painted floor welcomes visitors and invites passersby to stop and chat.

ABOVE Weatherproof rattan chairs and a glass-top table help create this stylish outdoor dining room.

In other areas, both sun and moisture can damage the goods. Select products specifically resistant to mold, mildew, and ultraviolet rays. Choices abound for products that work well in a protected outdoor environment. Here is some guidance on suitable outdoor products.

The market abounds with stylish outdoor furniture that works well in protected environments

Shades and blinds: Simple matchstick or rattan roll-up blinds have an unfussy, natural look and can protect furnishings from some rain and sun. Other treatments might include screens, lattice, and blinds that block ultraviolet rays while allowing breezes to waft through the space. Simply-made muslin curtains or canvas roll-up shades are decorative solutions that add privacy as well as beauty. (Cotton bed sheets are an inexpensive alternative to fabric by the yard.) If the fabric isn't fade resistant, though, the curtains can discolor.

Flooring and rugs: Tile, slate, concrete, and weather-resistant painted wood are natural floor choices that require minimal care. Soften the look and the feeling underfoot with natural-fiber rugs, such as sisal or hemp, which resist moisture damage; this type of floor covering works best in sheltered outdoor spaces.

Fabrics: Natural fabrics like muslin, ticking, or canvas are good accents for outdoor furniture. Choose subtle, earthy colors and patterns to blend—rather than clash—with your plants and flowers. Synthetics such as acrylics, vinyl-coated polyester, and laminated

LEFT A luxurious outdoor-seating platform is surrounded by muslin curtains that can be pulled closed when the wind blows or the sun is too strong.

THINK GREEN

Plastic Fantastic

Recycled materials are golden in the green world, especially plastic. Many companies are now making outdoor furniture out of recycled plastic water and milk bottles, detergent containers, and buckets. It's durable, can withstand the elements, and is available in cool styles.

BELOW Cushioned loveseats on this stone patio are pulled close for intimate conversation and the warmth of the fireplace.

cotton may resemble natural fabrics, but can be more weather resistant. Look for these fabrics at tent, awning, or fabric stores, as well as the porch and patio sections of department stores and pool-supply retailers. If the area is protected, you can use conventional fabrics without too much worry. Still, it's best to store cushions indoors when the forecast calls for rain. No matter what the fill material, once pillows and cushions have been soaked, they can take a long time to dry.

Decks and Patios

A well-designed deck or patio can add functional space to a house while serving as a transitional area between the interior of a home and the exterior property. By providing a defined surface for furniture and perhaps cooking equipment or storage, a deck or patio becomes an outdoor room. If you have the space, you may choose to combine both a deck and patio to increase the living area, or just one may serve your needs. Ask yourself how you intend to use your deck. Will it be for cooking and dining alfresco or used primarily as a sunning spot? How much money can you afford to spend on materials and

labor? Consider the pros and cons of doing at least some of the work yourself versus hiring a professional.

Because decks, patios, and terraces usually exist next to a house or adjoin a porch, they call for making the most efficient use of existing doors, windows, and steps. Creating workable traffic patterns is important, as you will sometimes be carrying trays full of food, beverages, pool equipment, and toys through the space. You have to organize furniture so that trips to and from the house are easy and take no longer than necessary, and you can maneuver through the space unencumbered.

Decide up front whether you need shaded areas as well as spots exposed to the sun. Where you position your space in relation to the shade provided by your house, trees, or other buildings will determine how much sun it gets. Awnings, umbrellas, pergolas, and even built-in trellises are good choices for sun protection and patios.

ABOVE This sunny patio area is defined by a stately vine-covered trellis.

Typically, a deck is located at the back of a house to provide the most privacy. If your lot is sloped, you might want to consider a multilevel deck. It not only offers a more gradual transition from the entry level to the ground, but also provides a way to create separate zones for different activities, such as barbecuing, dining, or sunning.

Railings are essential on raised decks, both for safety and for looks. So many attractive railing styles are available either as custom or standard elements that you can easily use railings to tie in the look of the deck to the architecture of your house.

THE GREEN DECK

Wood is the most eco-friendly deck-building product. It's biodegradable, produces few if any toxic byproducts, and is usually renewable. But it has negatives for the green builder. Many decks are made from old-growth varieties of wood, such as redwood and cedar, which can take hundreds of years to regenerate and often outpace responsible supply. Seek out lumber sources that are certified by the FSC, and you'll be assured that the wood is supplied from sources that can be reforested in a responsible way and that they have practiced efficient wood utilization. You can get more information about lumber labels on the FSC's consumer website. (See the Resource Guide on page 208.)

If you build a wood deck, it needs to be sealed periodically. Conventional oil- and water-based sealers for decks have high levels of toxic VOCs. Water-based sealers have lower levels of VOCs, but still contain petrochemical additives that can contribute

RIGHT Kicking off your shoes and curling up with a good book are just one of the pleasures of an outdoor room.

to air pollution. A more eco-friendly alternative is to use plant-oil preservatives, such as tung and linseed oil. They are most effective at protecting a wood deck when you use them annually.

Another green option is recycled plastic decking (RPL). RPL includes composite (half plastic, half wood dust, and some all-plastic products.) Be sure to check the percentage of recycled materials and the type of plastic used before you buy. The Healthy Building Network (see the Resource Guide on page 208) rates several well-known manufacturers of composite products as "less environmentally preferable." Some plastics, including vinyl and polystyrene, create human health risks during manufacturing and have limited options for recycling. Products that use recycled hard plastic (polyethylene) are environmentally preferable. RPL also has a higher price tag than most wood, but this is somewhat offset by its low maintenance requirements. A not-so-green aspect of composite RPL products is that they're not biodegradable and cannot be separated back into plastic and wood waste.

A common decking option is pressure-treated wood. In the past, wood was treated with chromated copper arsenate (CCA) to preserve it and make it resistant to rot and pests. Concerns about the

ABOVE An oversized grill set into a stone-top cooking and serving island invites good times on this backyard deck.

THINK GREEN

Plant a Tree

Besides their natural beauty, trees can also reduce your energy bill. Plant deciduous trees about 20 feet (6 meters) to the southeast and southwest of your home, and they will provide shade through the morning and afternoon in the summer. When the leaves drop, they will allow the sun's rays to warm your interior space.

RIGHT Fill up any unused corners on a patio with large, eye-catching plants.

dangers of arsenic prompted the phasing out of CCA lumber in 2004. However, CCA lumber may still be present in existing structures. If you're concerned, coating an older deck with a water-based paint or low-VOC sealant will reduce or eliminate exposure to CCA. Today's pressure-treated lumber processors have replaced arsenic with copper compounds, such as alkaline copper quaternary (ACQ). It consists of recycled copper that doesn't have any arsenic ingredients. Choose treated wood with a built-in water repellent and seal the deck periodically.

PATIOS

The most environmentally friendly option for outdoor living spaces is a patio rather than a deck. Because it is on the ground level, a patio uses fewer resources and materials. Patios are also easier to maintain and are more weather resistant than decks. When designing your patio, think of it as a defined space for the arrangement of furniture, a cooking area, and plantings. In addition, you can introduce an interesting shape, pattern, or texture to the landscape. As you would with any room, consider how your patio will affect your lifestyle. For example, if you'll be cooking outside, you'll need easy access to and from the kitchen.

Other practical matters will affect your plans. For drainage purposes, even a flat site will need some grading. If terraced into a steep slope, your patio will require a retaining wall. Before you

ABOVE LEFT Light-color decking mixes well with this home's exterior hue and the natural furnishings.

ABOVE RIGHT A dark wood stain blends with the colors of nature and enhances casual accessories. It needs to be sealed periodically to prevent fading.

ABOVE This outdoor space was personalized with as much attention to detail as an interior room.

proceed with paving or grading, refer to your property's site plans and follow local building codes. Your contractor will know that the site should slope away from the house for drainage, but might not be aware of the location of a septic system and any pipes that need to be avoided when excavating.

Outdoor Lighting

If you want to enjoy your outdoor living area after the sun goes down, you'll need some added lighting. You can of course opt for candles and torches, which create a warm, atmospheric glow. But you can't count on candles to supply the necessary light if the wind kicks up or the weather is questionable. Lighting is also a safety issue. An unlit stairway, path, or driveway can be dangerous at night. You have a few options. Aboveground, on-deck, and in-ground systems that utilize low-voltage lighting are available for installation by the average do-it-yourselfer.

Consider your lighting needs while you develop your overall landscape plan. That way, if you want a more complicated system,

LIVE WISE, LIVE WELL

Paving Particulars

You have many natural choices for the floor of your patio or garden room. For any of these paving solutions, the key to success is making sure that the surface you're paving is perfectly flat and prepared with a base of rough gravel and sand.

- **Brick:** For a warm and classic look, nothing beats brick. For paths and patios, use paving bricks. They are less likely than common bricks to crack and heave with the effects of winter weather and traffic.
- **Flagstone:** Sandstone, bluestone, limestone, slate, and granite complement just about any architectural style.
- **Pavers:** Concrete can be cast into molds to form individual pavers that mimic brick and cut stone. Strong, durable, and much less expensive than stone or brick, pavers are ideal for large areas.
- **Tile:** Terra-cotta, quarry, and glazed tile lends an Old World look to a garden and is a perfect paving solution for hot climates. If you don't live in a temperate area, use only those tiles that can withstand freezing temperatures and conditions, or limit your tiling to protected areas.
- **Gravel:** Loose materials, such as river stones, pea gravel, and crushed stones, are easy to work with and relatively inexpensive. The final result is an attractive and versatile look — gravel looks equally appropriate in an English-style garden, a Southwest desert garden, or an Asian garden.
- **Concrete:** While it might not seem like the most aesthetically pleasing solution, a cast-concrete patio has some distinct advantages and produces a very attractive floor. It's affordable, flat, and quick to install, and can provide a base for other paving materials later.

you'll be ready to have the electrical work done as your layout is being established. Have outdoor fixtures installed by a licensed electrician who will follow local building codes, has experience with outdoor wiring, and knows how deep to bury lines. Include several all-weather receptacles protected by ground-fault circuit interrupters (GFCIs) in the deck, patio, or porch areas. This will allow you to plug in strings of lights for special occasions as well as audio equipment and other electronic items. Be thoughtful of your neighbors—make sure neither light nor sound encroaches on their space. Don't go overboard with lighting, but do provide adequate transitional lighting from inside to outside, allowing eyes to adjust.

Eco-Smart Lighting

Because outdoor lighting fixtures often run for many hours, they can consume a lot of electricity. That's why it's important to look for energy-efficient options whenever possible.

A simple way to save energy is to limit the amount of time that the lights are used. Programmable timers let you set the on time for the

ABOVE These decorative sconces provide just the right amount of light to illuminate the path to and from the house.

lights. You can also purchase photocell units that will automatically make the lights come on only after the sun sets. Another option—especially for making yards or driveways more secure—are motion sensors. These automatically turn on lights for short periods of time when movement is detected.

When choosing outdoor lighting fixtures, look for low-energy options

Low-voltage lighting is a good choice to light up your landscape, sidewalks, plants, and the path from the house to your yard. It requires transformers to step the household current down to 15 volts or less and comes in kits that give you everything you need for installation. It's available at home centers and lighting stores, and it provides a low-budget way to add ambiance as well as provide safety to your landscape. A good eco-choice, it delivers light just where it's needed and uses less wattage than standard incandescent bulbs. Ask

LEFT This retro-style bamboo bar is a fun focal point on the backyard patio. A decorative light fixture continues the mood while adding a glow at night.

203

ABOVE A luxurious pool house has folding doors that open up to allow true indoor/outdoor living.

your home improvement store what kind of low-voltage kit is best for the kind of application you want.

Light-emitting diode bulbs (LEDs) are the way to go for security applications, such as floodlighting the front of the house. Because they use only a fraction of the energy of traditional incandescent lighting and last a long time, they're perfect for applications where lights may be on for extended periods. LEDs should be covered or shaded from the elements. Unlike CFLs, LEDs function even better in low temperatures, but check the label to see if the bulbs are suited for outdoor use.

You can also use solar energy to power your outdoor lights. During the day, small photovoltaic (PV) modules absorb sunlight and convert it into electricity that's stored in a battery in the light fixtures. These lights can be manual or equipped with motion sensors or light sensing controls. They don't emit a great deal of light, but they're effective enough to light up pathways or steps in the yard. Use PV-powered lights for areas that are not close to an existing power line. Installation is often as easy as pushing a stake-mounted fixture into the ground.

Landscaping

No outdoor space is completely successful unless it is complemented
and integrated with your landscape. You can enhance an area by
changing the landscape around it. You may want to plan a garden
around your patio, planting shrubs and flowers to highlight the site.

LEFT A concrete birdbath on a
pedestal is a stately backyard
accessory and a sure way to
attract a variety of birds to
the patio.

THINK GREEN

Green Landscaping

While you're landscaping your outdoor area, be sure to use these eco-friendly tips to help you use less water and fewer toxic substances.

- **Opt for organic.** Make your own mulch out of dead leaves, plants, branches, grass clippings, and fruit and vegetable scraps, and put it in garden beds and at the base of trees. When mulch is used, it stops moisture from evaporating, which reduces watering needs. Use organic fertilizer and avoid toxic pesticides.
- **Don't waste water.** Add a battery-operated timer to your sprinkler so you can turn on water for spurts of 15 to 20 minutes, giving the water time to soak into the soil. Some timers have settings for different days of the week and can be set to turn on sprinklers in different parts of the yard. Get a rainfall sensor and add it to your manual or automatic sprinkling system. It senses the moisture level of the soil and turns the sprinkler on only when the plants need it.
- **Go native.** Make sure trees, bushes, grass, and flowers in your yard are native to your area. They'll be more likely to thrive with minimal care and less water, fertilizer, and pesticides.
- **Use drip irrigation.** This is a system of plastic tubing that delivers water directly to the roots of plants. Because water is emitted into the soil rather than sprayed into the air, it cuts down on waste and maintains moisture levels. It's best for watering individual plants, shrubs, and trees.
- **Use recycled materials.** If you're putting in fences, decks, and furniture, look for recycled wood and other building materials at local salvage yards or reused building material stores. Visit *www.bmra.org* to find a store near you. If you can't reuse, look online to see what green building materials are available for your project.

By varying the shape, colors, and materials, you can introduce a note of interest or a focal point into the area. Most open spaces look best when they are defined by either hedges or fencing. Low plantings provide definition without impeding the view. Choices are nearly endless, ranging from clipped holly trees to low-growing junipers to a flower border of perennials or annuals. Consider what colors and fragrances you would like to have. A deck provides the perfect locale for a lush container garden, especially in an urban area where garden space is lacking. Be sure to choose plants that are suitable for the amount of light your deck receives.

LEFT The site for this outdoor living space and pool area is defined by lush plantings and a collection of oversized ceramic pots.

Resource Guide

The following list of manufacturers and associations is meant to be a general guide to additional industry and product-related sources. It is not intended as a listing of products and manufacturers represented by the photographs in this book.

Manufacturers

American Standard
www.americanstandard-us.com
800-442-1902
Manufactures plumbing and tile products.

Armstrong World Industries
www.armstrong.com
717-672-9611
Manufactures floors, cabinets, ceilings, and ceramic tiles.

Artemide
www.artemide.com
Manufactures lighting fixtures.

Bassett Furniture Industries
www.bassettfurniture.com
877-525-7070
Manufactures both upholstered furniture and casegoods.

Benjamin Moore & Co.
www.benjaminmoore.com
855-724-6802
Manufactures paint, including low-VOC options.

Couristan
www.couristan.com
800-223-6186
Manufactures natural and synthetic carpets and rugs.

Elmwood Reclaimed Timber
www.elmwoodreclaimedtimber.com
800-705-0705
Sells reclaimed timber and stone products.

Expanko Resilient Flooring
www.expanko.com
800-345-6202
Manufactures cork and rubber flooring.

Fisher & Paykel Appliances Ltd
www.fisherpaykel.com
888-936-7872
Manufactures kitchen appliances.

General Electric
www.ge.com
800-626-2005
Manufactures appliances and electronics.

Ginger
www.gingerco.com
949-417-5207
Manufactures lighting and
bathroom accessories.

Glidden
www.glidden.com
800-454-3336
Manufactures paints.

Globus Cork
www.corkfloor.com
718-742-7264
Manufactures cork flooring.

Green Mountain Soapstone Corporation
www.greenmountainsoapstone.com
802-468-5636
Manufactures soapstone floors, sinks,
and countertops.

Island Stone North America
www.islandstone.com
Manufactures natural stone and glass tiles.

Jian & Ling Bamboo
dave@jianlingbamboo.com
757-368-2060
Manufactures vertical- and horizontal-cut
bamboo flooring.

Kohler
www.kohler.com
800-456-4537
Manufactures plumbing products.

Sherwin-Williams
www.sherwinwilliams.com
800-474-3794
Manufactures paint and accessories,
including environmentally friendly products.

Teragren
www.teragren.com
800-929-6333
Manufactures bamboo flooring, panels,
veneers, and countertops.

Velux America
www.velux.com
800-888-3589
Manufactures skylights and solar tunnels.

Associations and Organizations

Building Materials Reuse Association
www.bmra.org
773-340-2672
A nonprofit educational organization
whose mission is to facilitate building
deconstruction and the reuse/recycling of
recovered building materials. Its website
provides a directory of businesses that
are members.

Efficient Windows Collaborative
www.efficientwindows.org
A nonprofit educational organization
that provides information about energy-
efficient windows.

Energy Star
www.energystar.gov
A program of the Environmental Protection
Agency that offers energy-efficient solutions.

Forest Stewardship Council (FSC)
www.us.fsc.org
612-353-4511
Establishes standards and issues certification
for sustainable forestry worldwide.

Healthy Building Network
www.healthybuilding.net
877-974-2767
A national network of green-building professionals dedicated to promoting healthier building materials.

Home Ventilating Institute
www.hvi.org
855-484-8368
A nonprofit association of the manufacturers of home ventilation products.

Kitchen Cabinet Manufacturers Association
www.kcma.org
703-264-1690
Helps cabinet manufacturers demonstrate their commitment to environmental sustainability and helps consumers easily identify environmentally friendly products.

National Fenestration Rating Council (NFRC)
www.nfrc.org
301-589-1776
Provides energy-performance ratings and other information about windows, skylights, and doors.

NSF International
www.nsf.org
800-673-8010
An independent not-for-profit organization committed to making the world a safer place for consumers.

The Freecycle Network
www.freecycle.org
A private nonprofit organization that gives away old items instead of discarding them in an effort to reduce waste, save resources, and ease the burden on landfills.

The Rainforest Alliance
www.smartwood.org
212-677-1900
Offers a diverse set of certification and verification services.

WaterSense
www.epa.gov/watersense
866-987-7367
A program sponsored by the Environmental Protection Agency to promote water-efficient products.

Glossary

Accent lighting A type of lighting that highlights an area or object to emphasize that aspect of a room's character.

Accessible designs Those that accommodate persons with physical disabilities.

Adaptable designs Those that can be easily changed to accommodate a person with disabilities.

Ambient lighting General illumination that surrounds a room. There is no visible source of the light.

Backlighting Illumination coming from a source behind or at the side of an object.

Backsplash The vertical part at the rear and sides of a countertop that protects the adjacent wall.

Biodegradable Capable of being broken down by living things and absorbed into the ecosystem.

Built-in Any element, such as a bookcase or cabinetry, that is built into a wall or an existing frame.

Candlepower The luminous intensity of a beam of light (total luminous flux) in a particular direction, measured in units called candelas.

Carbon footprint An estimated measure of the amount of carbon dioxide and other greenhouse gases emitted by businesses or organizations as part of their day-to-day operations or by individuals as part of their daily activities.

Clearance The amount of space between two fixtures, the centerlines of two fixtures, or a fixture and an obstacle, such as a wall.

Code A locally or nationally enforced mandate regarding structural design, materials, plumbing, or electrical systems that states what you can or cannot do when you build or remodel.

Compact fluorescent light (CFL) Bulbs that produce less heat and use reduced electricity; more energy-efficient than traditional lightbulbs.

Complementary colors Hues directly opposite each other on the color wheel. As the strongest contrasts, complements tend to intensify each other.

Contemporary Any modern design (after 1920) that does not contain traditional elements.

Daylighting The use of natural light from windows, skylights, and other openings to supplement or replace electric light in a home or building.

Dimmer switch A switch that can vary the intensity of the light it controls.

Ecosystem A set of living things interacting with one another and their physical environment, functioning as a unit.

Ecube A small wax cube placed in the refrigerator that mimics food; the cube is connected to the fridge's cooling system, which will respond to the wax's

rather than the air's temperature to conserve energy.

Embodied energy The amount of energy required to bring a product, material, or service to the point of use, including the energy used during extraction, manufacturing, packaging, transportation, assembly, and installation.

Energy efficiency Using less energy to accomplish the same task, in order to reduce air pollution and lower costs.

Energy Star rating The Environmental Protection Agency's labeling program that classifies and promotes energy-efficient products to reduce greenhouse gas emissions.

Essential oils Oils used for their aroma and for medicinal purposes. Natural essential oils can include oils made from lemons, peppermint leaves, lavender, and other plants.

Fair trade A trading partnership that seeks better social and environmental standards for disadvantaged producers and workers and advocates the fair payment for the purchase of their goods, particularly those exported from developing countries.

Fittings The plumbing devices that bring water to the fixtures.

Fluorescent bulb A glass tube coated on the interior with phosphor, a chemical compound that emits light when activated by ultraviolet energy. Air in the tube is replaced with a combination of argon gas and a small amount of mercury.

Focal point The dominant element in a room or design, usually the first to attract attention.

Fossil fuel Fuel formed in the earth from ancient (fossilized) plant or animal remains. Fossil fuels include coal, oil, and natural gas.

Global warming An increase in the earth's average atmospheric and oceanic temperatures that is believed to be the result of an increase in the greenhouse effect, resulting especially from pollution.

Gray water Household wastewater that does not contain serious contaminants.

Greenhouse gas Any gas that contributes to the greenhouse effect, which is the warming of the surface and atmosphere of the earth caused by conversion of solar radiation into heat.

Harmonious color scheme Also called analogous, a combination focused on neighboring hues on the color wheel.

High-efficiency particulate air (HEPA) filters Filters, typically found in vacuums and air-conditioning units, that are designed to remove more than 99 percent of harmful allergens from the air. They help reduce dust, mold spores, pet dander, and other allergens.

Hue Another term for specific points—that is, colors—on the pure, clear range of the color wheel.

Incandescent lighting A bulb (lamp) that converts electric power into light by passing electric current through a filament of tungsten wire.

Indirect lighting A subdued type of lighting that is not head-on, but rather reflected against another surface such as a ceiling.

LED lighting Long-lasting lighting that conserves electricity. LED stands for light-emitting diode.

LEED Abbreviation for Leadership in Energy and Environmental Design, a U.S. Green Building Council program that evaluates the environmental sustainability of buildings and certifies them based on the number of points earned.

Low flow Describes plumbing fixtures, such as faucets, toilets, and showerheads, that reduce water use by intensifying but decreasing volume of the flow.

Lumen The measurement of a source's light output—the quantity of visible light.

Lumens per watt (LPW) The ratio of the amount of light (lumens) provided to the energy (watts) used to produce the light.

Microfiber A nonabrasive synthetic material (a blend of polyester and polyamide) that removes dust, dirt, and grease from any hard surface, including mirrors and countertops, without streaking, scratching, or leaving lint.

Molding An architectural band used to trim a line where materials join or create a linear decoration. It is typically made of wood, plaster, or a polymer.

Occasional piece A small piece of furniture for incidental use, such as an end table.

Organic Relating to or derived from living organisms. Organic refers to the way agricultural products are produced and processed.

Organic cotton Cotton grown without pesticides or fertilizers and usually woven into textiles, such as bedding and towels.

Orientation The placement of any object or space, such as a window, door, or room, and its relationship to the points on a compass.

Passive solar Refers to capitalizing on the sun's energy to heat and cool living spaces naturally, without the use of mechanical or electrical devices.

Peninsula A countertop, with or without a base cabinet, that is connected at one end to a wall or another counter and extends outward, providing access on three sides.

Petrochemical A chemical derived from petroleum or natural gas. Products made from petrochemicals include plastics, detergents, solvents, and flooring and insulation materials.

Petroleum based Products that are created through a complex, energy-intensive process involving black crude oil that releases toxins into the air.

Phantom load The electricity used by TVs, coffeemakers, and other devices when they're turned off and drawing power from the outlet.

Photovoltaic (PV) Pertaining to the direct conversion of light into electricity. PV cells, or solar cells, are semiconductors that produce electrical energy when exposed to sunlight. PV energy generates electricity by absorbing light energy rather than burning fossil fuels, so it doesn't release any greenhouse gases.

Plant-based Products that are created using natural ingredients derived from plants.

Post-consumer waste Raw materials that have been used by consumers, recycled, and then morphed into something else.

Primary color A color that can't be produced in pigments by mixing other colors. The primary colors are red, blue, and yellow.

PVC A common thermoplastic resin used in a wide variety of products, including spray bottles, flooring, and siding.

R-value A measurement of a product's resistance to heat loss.

Secondary color A mixture of two primary colors. The secondary colors are orange, green, and purple.

Sectional Furniture made into separate pieces that coordinate with each other. The pieces can be arranged together as a large unit or independently.

Slipcover A fabric or plastic cover that can be draped or tailored to fit over a piece of furniture.

Sustainability The ability to meet the needs of the present without compromising the ability of future generations to meet their needs. A sustainable process is one that can be maintained indefinitely without a negative impact on the environment.

Task lighting Lighting that concentrates in specific areas for tasks, such as preparing food, applying makeup, reading, or doing crafts.

Tone Degree of lightness or darkness of a color.

Toxin A substance that can cause severe illness, poisoning, disease, or death when ingested, inhaled, or absorbed by the skin.

Track lighting Lighting that utilizes a fixed band that supplies a current to movable light fixtures.

Trompe l'oeil Literally meaning "fool the eye"; a painted mural that creates the illusion of realistic images and three-dimensional space.

Tufting The fabric of an upholstered piece or a mattress that is drawn tightly to secure the padding, creating regularly spaced indentations.

U-factor A measurement of the rate of heat transfer through a product.

Uplight Light or a fixture that is directed upward toward the ceiling.

Valance Short drapery that hangs along the top of a window, with or without a curtain underneath it.

Value In relation to a scale of grays ranging from black to white, the lightness (tint) or darkness (shade) of a color.

Vanity A bathroom floor cabinet that usually contains a sink and storage space.

Veneer High-quality wood that is cut into very thin sheets for use as a surface material.

Volatile organic compounds (VOCs) Chemicals containing carbon at a molecular level that easily form vapors and gases at room temperature.

Wainscoting A wall covering of boards, plywood, or paneling that covers the lower section of an interior wall and usually contrasts with the wall surface above it.

Work triangle The area in a kitchen bounded by the lines that connect the sink, range, and refrigerator.

Photo and Designer Credits

All photography by Karyn R. Millet unless otherwise noted. **Front cover:** design: Sheldon Harte **back cover:** design: James Radin **page 2:** design: Ken Fulk **page 5:** design: Sheldon Harte **page 7:** design: Ken Fulk **page 9:** design: Deborah Wachter **pages 11–13:** *all* design: M2 Design **page 14:** design: Sheldon Harte **page 15:** design: Katrin Cargill and Carol Glasser **page 16:** architect: Mark Whitman **page 17:** design: James Radin **pages 19–20:** *both* design: Deborah Wachter **page 21:** design: Bonesteel Trout Hall **page 22:** design: Sheldon Harte **pages 25–26:** *both* design: Katrin Cargill and Carol Glasser **page 27:** design: Bonesteel Trout Hall **pages 28–29:** *all* design: James Radin **page 32:** design: M2 Design **pages 33–35:** *both* design: Bonesteel Trout Hall **page 36:** design: Chad Eisner **page 37:** design: Bonesteel Trout Hall **pages 38–39:** *both* design: M2 Design **page 41:** *both* design: M2 Design **page 42:** design: Karin Cusack **page 43:** design: Bonesteel Trout Hall **page 44:** design: Molly Isaksen **page 45:** design: The One and Only Pamilla **page 46:** design: M2 Design **pages 48–51:** *all* design: Sheldon Harte **page 52:** design: Bonesteel Trout Hall **page 53:** design: James Radin **page 55:** *left* design: Club Cascadas; *right* design: James Radin **pages 56–57:** *both* Katrin Cargill and Carol Glasser **page 58:** design: James Radin **page 61:** design: Bonesteel Trout Hall **page 62:** design: Barbara King **page 63:** design: Karen Harautuneian, Hub of the House **page 64:** design: Chad Eisner **page 67:** design: Gabriel Gelbart and Paul Rhoadzhagen **page 70:** design: Bonesteel Trout Hall **page 71:** design: William F. Holland **page 72:** design: Bonesteel Trout Hall **page 73:** *top* design: James Radin; *bottom* design: Bonesteel Trout Hall **page 74:** design: Sheldon Hate **page 75:** design: Bonesteel Trout Hall **page 76:** *both* design: Sheldon Harte **page 77:** design: Barbara King **page 78:** design: Bonesteel Trout Hall **page 79:** design: Joan Behnke **page 81:** design: Ken Fulk **page 82:** design: Kari Cusack **pages 83–84:** *both* design: M2 Design **page 85:** design: Chad Eisner **page 87:** design: Bonesteel Trout Hall **page 90:** design: Katrin Cargill and Carol Glasser **page 91:** design: Sheldon Harte **page 93:** design: Bonesteel Trout Hall **page 94:** design: William F. Holland **page 96:** design: Ken Fulk **page 97:** design: Barbara King **page 98:** design: Sheldon Harte **page 103:** design: M2 Design **page 104:** *left* design: Chris Eisner; *right* design: Walnut Wallpaper **pages 105–106:** *both* design: Katrin Cargill and Carol Glasser **page 107:** design: Sheldon Harte **page 108:** design: Chad Eisner **page 109:** design: The Warwick Group **page 110:** design: Ken Fulk **page 111:** design: M2 Design **page 113:** design: Katrin Cargill and Carol Glasser **pages 114–115:** *both* design: Kari Cusack **pages 116–117:** *both* design: Bonesteel Trout Hall **pages 118–121:** *both* design: Carla Smith, Hub of the House **page 122:** design: Katrin Cargill and Carol Glasser **page 123:** design: Sheldon Harte **page 124:** design: Kari Cusack **page 125:** design: William F. Holland **page 126:** design: Katrin Cargill and Carol Glasser **page 127:** design: Ken Fulk **page 128:** design: Bonesteel Trout Hall **page 129:** *left* design: Karen Harautuneian, Hub of the House; *right* design: Tim Barber, Inc. **page 130:** *left* design: Karen Harautuneian, Hub of the House; *right* design: Portobello Road **page 131:** design: Chad Eisner **pages 132–133:** *both* design: William F. Holland **page 134:** design: Karen Harautuneian, Hub of the House **page 135:** design: William F. Holland **page 136:** design: The Warwick Group **page 137:** design: M2 Design **page 138:** design: Karen Harautuneian, Hub of the House **page 139:** design: Kari Cusack **pages 140–141:** *both* courtesy of Kohler **page 142:** *left* design: Woodson

& Rummerfield; *right* design: James Radin **page 143:** design: M2 Design **page 144:** design: William F. Holland **page 145:** design: Chad Eisner **page 146:** courtesy of Kitchens By Deane **page 147:** design: Sheldon Harte **page 149:** design: The Warwick Group **page 150:** *bottom* design: The Warwick Group **page 151:** design: Sheldon Harte **page 153:** design: The Warwick Group **page 154:** courtesy of Italian Trade Commission **page 155:** design: James Radin **page 156:** design: Sheldon Harte **pages 158–160:** *all* design: Bonesteel Trout Hall **page 161:** design: Deborah Wachter **page 162:** design: M2 Design **pages 163–164:** *both* design: The Warwick Group **page 167:** design: Bonesteel Trout Hall **page 168:** design: James Radin **page 170:** design: Kari Cusack **page 171:** design: Bonesteel Trout Hall **page 172:** design: James Radin **page 173:** design: William F. Holland **page 174:** design: James Radin **page 175:** design: Ken Fulk **page 176:** courtesy of Renaissance Conservatories **pages 178–180:** *both* design: Bonesteel Trout Hall **page 181:** design: Kari Cusack **page 182:** design: Bonesteel Trout Hall **page 183:** *top* design: Bonesteel Trout Hall; *bottom* courtesy of DalTile **page 184:** courtesy of Crossville, Inc. **page 185:** design: Gabriel Gelbart and Paul Rhoadzhagen **page 186:** design: Kari Cusack **page 187:** design: M2 Design **page 188:** design: Lowenthal Residence **page 190:** design: Patricia Benner Landscape Design **page 191:** design: Deborah Wachter **page 192:** design: Patricia Benner Landscape Design **page 193:** design: Bonesteel Trout Hall **page 194:** design: Paul Hendershot **page 195:** design: Joan Behnke & Associates **pages 196–197:** *both* design: Patricia Benner Landscape Design **page 198:** design: Andrew Virtue **page 199:** *left* design: Marquis; *right* design: Paul Hendershot **page 200:** design: Joan Behnke & Associates **page 202:** courtesy of Cascades **page 203:** design: Bonesteel Trout Hall **page 204:** design: Kari Cusack **page 205:** design: Barbara Milo Ohrbach **pages 207–209:** *both* design: Bonesteel Trout Hall **page 219:** architect: Mark Whitman **page 221:** design: Sheldon Harte

Index